USING ART TO TEACH READING COMPREHENSION STRATEGIES

USING ART TO TEACH READING COMPREHENSION STRATEGIES

LESSON PLANS FOR TEACHERS

Jennifer Klein and Elizabeth Stuart

Published in partnership with the
National Art Education Association

ROWMAN & LITTLEFIELD EDUCATION
Lanham, Maryland • New York • Toronto • Plymouth, UK
2013

Published in partnership with the National Art Education Association

Published in the United States of America
by Rowman & Littlefield Education
A division of Rowman & Littlefield Publishers, Inc.
A wholly owned subsidiary of The Rowman & Littlefield Publishing Group, Inc.
4501 Forbes Boulevard, Suite 200, Lanham, Maryland 20706
www.rowman.com

10 Thornbury Road, Plymouth PL6 7PP, United Kingdom

British Library Cataloguing in Publication Information Available

Library of Congress Cataloging-in-Publication Data

Klein, Jennifer, 1959-
    Using art to teach reading comprehension strategies : lesson plans for teachers / Jennifer Klein and
Elizabeth Stuart
        p. cm.
    Includes bibliographical references.
    ISBN 978-1-4758-0153-8 (pbk. : alk. paper)—ISBN 978-1-4758-0154-5 (electronic) 1. Reading
(Primary) 2. Art in education. 3. Lesson planning. I. Stuart, Elizabeth, 1976- II. Title.
    LB1525.4.K54 2013
    372.4—dc23

                                                                                                                    2012031164

∞™ The paper used in this publication meets the minimum requirements of
American National Standard for Information Sciences—Permanence of Paper for
Printed Library Materials, ANSI/NISO Z39.48-1992.
Manufactured in the United States of America.

CONTENTS

PREFACE

One of the most exciting aspects of teaching for us is when we can collaboratively work with a group of colleagues to design and implement lessons that motivate, engage, challenge, and inspire children to learn. It is even more exciting when the experience builds on our passions. In our case, it was literacy and the arts. Not only did using the arts to teach reading comprehension strategies bring our passions together, the arts provided the opportunity for children to learn about the comprehension strategies in a text-free environment before applying the strategies to text. We feel very fortunate to have had the opportunity to collaborate with each other to develop and implement art/literacy integrated lessons and wanted to share our experience and ideas with other educators.

In our work, we saw how the arts helped engage the children whom we worked with, so we began to present our ideas at state and national conventions. As we continued to develop more lessons, we received so much positive feedback from colleagues, conference attendees, and parents that we wanted to put our work together in a resource so that other educators could use the lessons and ideas presented in our book to teach art/literacy integration lessons.

A major idea behind the book is that art can be a critical tool in helping students develop and refine reading strategies. This book explores how to teach reading comprehension strategies through art. In our extensive work on this topic, we have found that when reading strategies are presented in the context of art first, the students are better able to incorporate these tools into their reading. This book provides both grade-level and art teachers with an overview of six different reading strategies and integrated reading and art lessons that can be implemented in your own classrooms and schools.

Targeted for elementary teachers, this book is ideally designed so that grade-level and art teachers work collaboratively. We intentionally wrote this book to be as clear as possible for grade-level teachers who may not have a degree in art education. We understand that not every school has a dedicated visual arts instructor, and we believe all the art lessons in this book can be taught by a grade-level teacher, reading specialist, or art teacher. This teacher-friendly, easy-to-use book offers background information on the strategies and lessons that allow you to copy student materials and begin implementing this approach in your classrooms right away.

These ideas began at Takoma Park Elementary School, in Montgomery County, Maryland, where we worked together, and grew out of our love and passion for the arts and the need to develop lessons that explicitly taught children reading comprehension strategies.

BACKGROUND OF THE PROJECT

Montgomery County Public Schools is the largest school system in the state of Maryland and the seventeenth-largest school system in the United States. It borders Washington, D.C., and has over 146,000 students in 201 schools. We have a 13 percent ESOL population, and 40.9 percent of our students participate in Free and Reduced-Price Meals System (FARMS). We have a 90 percent graduation rate, and our schools are frequently ranked as some of the top schools in the country.

In 2000, the superintendent of Montgomery County Public Schools (MCPS) began an initiative to place a staff development teacher in each one of our schools. The purpose of the staff development teacher was to bring the county initiatives into the schools, train teachers, and provide on-site staff development. During this first year of the project, in addition to implementing county-wide initiatives, schools were encouraged to identify individual school needs and provide staff development to meet those needs. Takoma Park Elementary was one of 136 elementary schools in MCPS. This is where our project began.

Takoma Park Elementary School (TPES) is a unique primary (K–2) school. It is located in Takoma Park, Maryland, which borders Washington, D.C. In 2002, TPES offered the following:

- Primary school: Head Start, kindergarten, first grade, and second grade
- Title I
- Books for Breakfast
- School community-based program
- Gifted and talented magnet for science and social studies
- Program of Assessment, Diagnosis, and Instruction (PADI)
- Yearly curriculum night and art showcase

The City of Takoma Park had 16,715 residents as of the 2010 census. These citizens are unusually diverse in age, ethnicity, language, economic condition, and length of residence. The city is also the home of many writers, musicians, and artists. The Takoma Park community is very environmentally conscious, and the residents are strong arts advocates.

Our Project Begins

One of the goals of the MCPS staff development project in 2002 and today focuses on bringing grade-level teams together to improve teaching and learning. In a collaborative atmosphere, some of the team's work includes reviewing curriculum, participating in book studies, analyzing data, and discussing children's needs during team meetings.

During the first year of our staff development project, the TPES staff participated in a book study. We read *Mosaic of Thought* (Keene & Zimmerman, 2007) and *Strategies That Work* (Harvey & Goudvis, 2007). Grade-level teams met during the school day to discuss each comprehension strategy and ways to teach the strategy to children. Many of our reading lessons grew out of our discussions from the lesson ideas and information presented in these books.

Using *Mosaic of Thought* and *Strategies That Work* as resources, we studied the following comprehension strategies:

- Making connections
- Questioning
- Visualizing
- Inferring
- Determining importance
- Synthesizing

Lisa Stuart (former TPES art teacher), Peggy Feeney (former TPES staff developer), and Jennifer Klein (former TPES reading specialist) met to design lessons that would use art to teach the comprehension strategies. Peggy brought forth the idea that to "comprehend something is to understand something" no matter what subject matter is being studied. Building on the idea that comprehension involves understanding, we looked for ways to use art to teach the different comprehension strategies.

Involving the Specialists

As part of the staff development project, the principal of Takoma Park Elementary School, Janet Dunn, asked us to work together to create a rotational integrated reading and art class. She wanted all the first and second graders in the school to rotate through a thirty-minute art class in addition to their regular art period, which was put in the schedule two times per week. She wanted the art teacher, the staff development teacher, and the reading specialist to work with the grade-level teachers to develop lessons that directly supported their reading curriculum. We decided to use reading comprehension strategies as the basis for these lessons. That year we focused on visualizing, questioning, and inferring. Once lessons were developed, we taught the art lessons in the art room and followed up with reading/language arts lessons in the reading classroom. We taught each lesson in the art room first because it offered a "text-free" environment. We believed that if we taught the strategy first in art, children would be able to learn the strategy and then be able to apply the strategy to text.

In subsequent years, the two of us moved on to different schools, but we continued to create lessons for synthesizing, determining importance, and making connections, and we taught them to the students in those schools. In the summer of 2008, we created a summer class for second graders called Art and Reading. There were ten kids in this weeklong class, and we focused on a different reading strategy each day.

The list below outlines the strategies we focused on each day of our summer program.

Day 1: Visualizing—Making pictures in your mind

Day 2: Making connections—How does the piece of art/story connect to me?

Day 3: Inferring—What the piece tells us and what we know = our meaning

Day 4: Determining importance—What is important in this piece of art/story? How can you tell?

Day 5: Asking questions—What do I wonder about this piece of art/story? What are my questions?

WHY IS THIS BOOK IMPORTANT NOW?

36% of subjects reported decreasing art content from their curricula due to increased demands to include language arts and math content in its place in their curricula.

No Child Left Behind: A Study of Its Impact on Art Education
(F. Robert Sabol, President, NAEA, 2010)

While we do not suggest that this book by any means should replace art instruction, the lesson ideas can support both art and reading indicators and standards. We designed the book so that lessons can be taught collaboratively between an art and reading teacher to support the reading/language arts program. In an ideal world, we believe that students should be receiving full art instruction in addition to the extra support outlined in the book. However, the data show that in some cases art teachers are required to infuse reading/language arts and math into their curriculum. This book enables art teachers to stay true to the national visual art standards, teach the art concepts and skills every elementary student needs, and integrate reading comprehension strategies in a meaningful way.

It is our goal that in reading this book you will feel the same passion that we do about infusing art into reading or vice versa. We can attest to the fact that, by teaching comprehension strategies though art first, students learn the strategies more easily and retain the information longer. The ideas presented in the following chapters are by no means exhaustive. We hope to spark your imagination and encourage you to change these lessons—make them your own, based on your comfort level with either subject. Good luck on your journey!

INTRODUCTION

According [...] future belongs to the following kinds of people—
"creators an[...] attern recognizers, and meaning makers. These
people—artis[...] ners, storytellers, caregivers, consolers, big pic-
ture thinkers—[...] ty's richest rewards and share its greatest joys."

A Whole New Mind (Pink, 2006, p. 1)

This book provides t[...] rated literacy and art lessons that they can use right away in their cl[...] the following comprehension strategies: making connections, questionin[...] ermining importance, inferring, and synthesizing. Each chapter focuses [...] tegies, defines each strategy, and provides classroom-tested lessons and i[...] strategies through the visual arts in order to improve reading comprehens[...].

WHY USE ART TO TEACH RE[...] REHENSION?

Children learn best when they can touc[...] Using art to teach comprehension strategies allows children to use multiple[...] n and, most importantly, apply the strategies in a text-free environment be[...] strategies to text. Comprehension skills can be very challenging for some[...] he skills needed for reading comprehension are taught first through the visual [...], children will be better equipped to apply the strategies to reading. In addition, many children are very motivated by art.

In our work, we have found that for many children art grabs their interest, art is motivating, and art is safe. Most children have something to say about a piece of art, and that

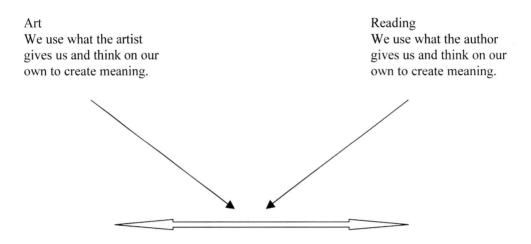

Art
We use what the artist
gives us and think on our
own to create meaning.

Reading
We use what the author
gives us and think on our
own to create meaning.

Art may provide the scaffolding children need to move from a text-free environment to a
text environment. The connection between art and text becomes natural.

Figure I.1.   Connection between Art and Reading.

is why starting with art is smart. Once the strategies of making connections, questioning,
visualizing, determining importance, inferring, and synthesizing are developed through
looking at and discussing art, children are better equipped to transfer the strategies to text.
This is the premise of our book.

The lessons found here support learners by teaching children to be metacognitive
(thinking about their own thinking) by showing them how to activate their own thinking
when analyzing art and, later, pieces of text. Figure I.1 explains why the visual arts can be
a good avenue for teaching children comprehension strategies. Once children understand
that comprehension is making meaning out of what they see or experience, they can apply
these strategies to reading in order to create meaning from what they have read.

Figure I.1 explains the connections between art and reading.

INTEGRATION OF THE ARTS

There are many approaches to arts-integrated instruction. The Kennedy Center's CETA
program (Changing Education Through the Arts) in Washington, D.C., defines arts integration as "an approach to teaching in which students construct and demonstrate their
understanding through an art form. Students engage in a creative process, which connects an art form and another subject area and meets evolving objectives in both" (www
.kennedy-center.org/education/ceta/arts_integration_definition.pdf).

Arts integration is not merely playing music in class or having students draw in class. It
is objective(s) in one art form (i.e., music, art, theatre, or dance) matched with objective(s)
in another subject area (e.g., math) and taught together in a meaningful way, making

strong connections. The lessons in the book address the National Visual Arts Standards, the Common Core Standards for English and Language Arts, and the National Reading Standards. Because of this, each chapter contains true examples of arts integration lessons.

HOW TO USE THIS BOOK

This book will increase your own understanding of comprehension strategies. If it is used as a material for a workshop, teachers will gain a deeper understanding of the comprehension strategies and of arts integration. The following collaboration models explained in the book will outline how teachers can collaborate in schools:

> Model 1: Where the classroom and art teacher can collaboratively work together, or if collaboration is not possible,
>
> Model 2: Where the classroom teacher can integrate art lessons into the reading/language arts block, or
>
> Model 3: Where the art teacher can integrate reading/language arts into the art program.

Each of the six chapters focuses on one of the strategies and follows a similar organization. Every chapter:

- addresses specific National Visual Arts Standards, Common Core Standards for Reading, and National Reading Standards;
- defines each strategy;
- explains why art is a good way to teach the strategy;
- provides lessons that explain how to teach the strategies in art;
- provides lessons that show how to teach children to apply these strategies to reading;
- includes a reflection from the writers;
- provides literacy benefits; and
- includes art and text resources.

Readers can choose to read the book in its entirety or jump from chapter to chapter to learn more about a certain strategy. The design of the book allows teachers to read about a strategy over the weekend and be ready to teach the lessons to the children the following week.

RESEARCH ON READING COMPREHENSION

For our project, we used multiple resources. We used the following two texts for our school book study: *Mosaic of Thought* (Keene & Zimmermann, 2007) and *Strategies That Work*

(Harvey & Goudvis, 2007). These books were very helpful in explaining how children learn to be metacognitive, which is the foundation for all comprehension, and drove our book study on reading comprehension strategies. We also began reading other books that dealt with arts integration, such as *Weaving through Words* (Mantione & Smead, 2003) and *Champions of Change: The Impact of the Arts on Learning* (Fiske, 1999).

In addition, we used the book *Revisit/Reflect/Retell* (Hoyt, 2008) because it offers teachers many different templates to use to check children's comprehension through writing and *Reading with Meaning: Teaching Comprehension in the Primary Grades* (Miller, 2002), which delves deeper into strategy instruction for primary grades. Our book is unique because it is the first that combines teaching the reading strategies through the visual arts. Please see page 107 for a full list of resources we think you will enjoy.

EXPLICIT TEACHING OF READING COMPREHENSION STRATEGIES

Many studies were done in the 1990s that supported using the explicit teaching model for strategy instruction and focused on why strategy instruction and teaching children to be metacognitive was important to improving comprehension. Building on the research by Dole, Duffy, Roehler, and Pearson (1991), Fielding and Pearson (1994), Gallager and Pearson (1983), Duffy et al. (1987), Duffy, Roehler, and Herrmann (1988), and Harvey et al. (1996) we developed our lessons using the explicit teaching model.

The thinking behind the research is that students need to:

1. Understand the strategy (introduction of the strategy)
2. See the strategy being modeled (modeling)
3. Have time to practice the strategy (guided practice)
4. Have time to apply the strategy independently (independent practice)
5. Allow time to share their thinking (sharing)

Using this format allows teachers to use the gradual release model, checking student understanding along the way.

TWENTY-FIRST-CENTURY SKILLS

According to The Partnership for 21st Century Skills, learning and innovation skills are what separate students who are prepared for increasingly complex life and work environments in the 21st century, from those who are not. A focus on creativity, critical thinking, communication, and collaboration is essential to prepare students for the future.

Partnership for 21st Century Skills (P21)

The ideas in this book utilize the following learning and innovation skills:

- Creativity and innovation
- Critical thinking and problem solving
- Communication and collaboration

NATIONAL AND COMMON CORE STANDARDS

To meet the needs of a wider audience both in the United States and abroad, we have included both the Common Core College and Career Readiness Anchor Standards for Reading and the National Reading Standards because we realize that throughout the world, curriculum may be based on either of these standards. The lessons in each chapter are also aligned with the National Visual Arts Standards.

The following additional standards can be met by incorporating artwork and texts that represent different cultures. Teachers can choose artwork, stories, dramas, poems, and myths from diverse cultures and time periods.

- Visual Arts Content Standard 4: Understanding the visual arts in relation to history and cultures
- Reading:
  - Common Core State Standards: In "Note on range and content of student reading" (on page 10 of the College and Career Readiness Anchor Standards for Reading), from the Common Core State Standards for English Language Arts & Literacy in History/Social Studies, Sciences, and Technical Subjects, students are encouraged to read a variety of stories, dramas, poems, and myths from diverse cultures and time periods. Students are also encouraged to read texts from other disciplines, which allows them to become better readers in all content areas.
  - National Reading Standard 9: Students develop an understanding of and respect for diversity in language use, patterns, and dialects across cultures, ethnic groups, geographic regions, and social roles.

TARGET AUDIENCE: ELEMENTARY GRADES 1–5

This book is uniquely designed to support the elementary-age reader who may be struggling with reading comprehension or as a way to introduce reading strategies to all students in a creative and engaging way. Most of the lessons in this book are geared for first through fifth graders. However, some kindergarten students who are ready to learn reading strategies may benefit from these lessons. Likewise, some middle-school students who are really struggling with reading comprehension will also benefit. Because synthesis is a more complex skill, we recommend this chapter for third through fifth graders and middle-school students. Ultimately, it is you the teacher who will need to choose which chapters will be most helpful for your students, depending on the strengths and weaknesses of each individual child.

We suggest you examine your class/school data to determine which areas of comprehension your students need the most support in and start there. Ideally, you would teach all these lessons if you have the time because even if your students have a firm grasp of the strategy, teaching it to them in a new way can further support them and deepen their understanding.

ELEMENTS OF ART AND PRINCIPLES OF DESIGN

In all the art lessons we refer frequently to the elements of art and principles of design. These are the building blocks for art that are taught starting in preschool. For your reference, all the elements of art and principles of design are listed and defined here. You may want to create or purchase posters to display around your room. Refer to them as you are teaching the art lessons in this book. There are several companies that sell these in sets (www.crystalproductions.com). There is a lot of information about the elements of art and principles of design in books and on the Internet. Here is some basic information to get you started.

Elements of Art

- *Line*: thick, thin, wavy, loopy, zigzag, straight, diagonal, horizontal, vertical, and so on
- *Color*: the use of hue
  - Primary colors: red, yellow, blue
  - Secondary colors: orange, green, purple
  - Warm colors: reds, oranges, yellows
  - Cool colors: blues, greens, purples
  - Complementary colors: colors that are across from each other on the color wheel
  - Tint: a color mixed with white
  - Shade: a color mixed with black
- *Shape*: geometric and organic (free-form)
- *Texture*: the way something feels (visual texture is implied texture)
- *Form*: three-dimensional shape (cube, pyramid, sphere, cylinder, etc.)
- *Space*: distances around, between, or within components of a work of art
  - Negative space: the area around an object
  - Positive space: the object itself

- ° Foreground: the part of the picture that is represented nearest to the viewer
- ° Middle ground: the space between the foreground and the background in the picture plane
- ° Background: the parts of an artwork that seem to be farthest away
- *Value*: lightness or darkness of a color

Principles of Design

- *Pattern/Repetition*: reoccurring objects
- *Contrast*: difference in color
- *Balance*: (visual balance) no space takes away from the whole
- *Rhythm*: visual beat (patterns and repetition used in a rhythmic way)
- *Movement*: keeps the eye traveling through the artwork
- *Unity*: harmony, elements in balance
- *Emphasis*: focal point

OBTAINING ARTWORK

There are multiple sources for finding artwork to use for the lessons in this book.

- Postcards: Art museums sell smaller reproductions of artwork that children can use at their tables or desks.
- Note cards: Many companies use artists' work on note cards that can be cut up and used in the classroom.
- Calendars: There are lots of yearly calendars containing master artists' work that you can cut up. Visit your local bookstore or calendar kiosk in the mall. Calendars generally go on sale in January.
- Print reproductions: Shorewood Educational online is one of the easiest ways to get large reproductions for whole-class discussions (www.artforschools.com).
- Art gallery: Visit your local art gallery, where you may be able to collect more resources.
- Digital reproductions: There are multiple ways to get images to project via LCD projector or Promethean/Smart board. Images can be purchased through companies (e.g., www.davisart.com) or pulled off the Internet (for educational use only) by doing an image search in your favorite web browser. Also, the National Gallery of Art has a database of open-access images that anyone can use (www.images.nga.gov).

MAKING CONNECTIONS

Connecting the Known to the Unknown

The meaning you get from a piece is intertwined with the meaning you bring to it.

7 Keys to Comprehension
(Zimmermann & Hutchins, 2003, p. 45)

A child is much more apt to remember stories, books, and incidents that are meaningful because they connect to other things in his life.

7 Keys to Comprehension
(Zimmermann & Hutchins, 2003, p. 57)

According to experts in the field of reading education, reading is a very "active" process. Children use what they already know to understand and make sense out of what they read. Good readers are constantly making connections between their own background knowledge (schema) and the texts they read; connections between texts; and connections between ideas presented in a text and the world. It is through these connections that children gain a deeper understanding of the text, of authors, and of community/world issues. Keene and Zimmermann (2007, pp. 100–101) group the types of connections children make before, during, and after reading into three categories:

- Text to self connections
- Text to text connections
- Text to world connections

Text to self connections are connections readers make between their own background knowledge and the setting, characters, or events in a story/text that help them to understand the text better. Thinking about what you already know about a topic can help you to bring your experiences to the text and as a result have a deeper understanding of what you read. Teaching children to activate their prior knowledge before, during, and after reading helps children to make connections to the story. To help children make this type of connection, teachers can ask questions such as: Has anything happened to you like this? Have you ever been to _____? What was it like? Making connections helps students to hold on to information because they are connecting the known to the unknown. In some cases, a child's background knowledge may be tied to emotional responses, and researchers in the field of memory note that emotional responses can be very strong and may contribute to remembering story elements.

Text to text connections are connections children make between two separate texts based on similarities in setting, characters, events, problems, solutions, and themes. Text to text connections can also be the connections children make between texts written by the same author, such as Tomie dePaola, Eric Carle, or Faith Ringgold. Text to text connections help children to identify an author's craft or style, similarities and differences between characters in the texts, and/or how the illustrations are similar. These connections can also help children understand recurring themes throughout books.

Text to world connections are connections children make between the events they read about and the events that occur in their own community or world. Perhaps a character in the story reminds them of a leader in their school, community, or world. Or they may make a connection between a setting in a story and a place they have visited. What they know about a place can help them make connections to the story, which will aid them in remembering details. For example, if a child has been to a certain geological area such as the Southwest and a poem or story is about the Southwest, the child can bring what he knows about the geography of the Southwest to better understand the story. Many times authors write about problems children experience at home or school. This allows children to make connections between the world of fiction and their world. At times, they can bring what they learn in a story to help them to solve a problem in their own life, such as friendship issues, environmental issues, school issues, or in some cases, having to deal with an animal death or aging grandparent. These connections help children better understand their world.

Why Making Connections?

Making connections is a necessary skill for comprehending text and understanding author craft, recurring themes, and understanding the world. Making connections:

- engages students in text and allows them to use their background knowledge while reading to deepen their comprehension;

- requires children to be active readers as they think about how the text connects to them, other texts, and their community/world;
- helps children make sense of the world around them;
- teaches children how to solve problems by examining how characters solve problems in the stories they read; and
- provides the basis for author studies. (An author study is when three or more books by the same author are reviewed to observe the similarities and differences between characters, setting, problem, solution, and author craft.)

Things to Remember

Children will need time to work on making connections. At first children may make surface connections or connections that do not really deepen comprehension. They will need guidance as you teach them that it is the connections they make about characters, setting, problems, solutions, events, and messages that are the important connections that will lead to a deeper understanding of the text.

Why Art and Making Connections?

Explicit strategy instruction is essential in teaching children to make connections, especially for children who are having difficulty with comprehension. Using art as the stimulus, teachers can model each of the three connections by modeling think-alouds and then providing guided and independent practice as children articulate and explain their connections. By teaching the strategy through artwork first, children learn to make connections with a visual prompt (the piece of art) prior to being required to connect to the printed word. Many children are able to respond easily to what they can see in pictures. In addition, because there is often no "right" or "wrong" answer when interpreting art, some children are more relaxed connecting to art than to text, creating an environment where they feel free to take risks. After children understand how to make connections through art, text can be introduced, and those skills can be easily transferred.

TEACHING THE MAKING CONNECTIONS STRATEGY THROUGH ART

National Visual Arts Standards

The following art content standards are addressed in the art lessons in this chapter:

Content standard 1: Understanding and applying media, techniques, and processes
Content standard 3: Choosing and evaluating a range of subject matter, symbols, and ideas

Content standard 4: Understanding the visual arts in relation to history and cultures
Content standard 5: Reflecting on and assessing the characteristics and merits of their work and the work of others
Content standard 6: Making connections between visual arts and other disciplines

Time Frame

Five twenty- to thirty-minute class periods

Art Vocabulary

- *Elements of art*: line, color, shape, texture, form, space, and value
- *Principles of design*: pattern, repetition, contrast, balance, rhythm, movement, unity, and emphasis

Artists/Artworks

Choose artwork that you feel children can relate to on a personal level and artwork that portrays your geographical location (e.g., climate, landforms, points of interest, bodies of water).

- Bearden, Romare. *The Block*, 1971
- Homer, Winslow. *The Gulf Stream*, 1899
- Hopper, Edward. *Tables for Ladies*, 1930
- Jackson, Alexander Young. *The Red Maple*, 1914
- Lange, Dorothea. *Migrant Mother*, 1936
- Laurence, Jacob. *The Migration Series*, 1940–1941
- Picasso, Pablo. *The Tragedy*, 1903

Materials

- Large reproductions of artwork (see "Resources" for suggestions)
- Small reproductions of artwork (place fifty to one hundred at each table)
- Capture sheets (three)
- Pencils
- Chart paper
- Markers
- Crayons
- Colored pencils

- 9-inch × 12-inch white paper (two sheets for each student)
- A variety of natural objects (e.g., shells, pinecones, small braches, leaves, flowers)

Session 1: Connecting Art to Art

Time Frame

One thirty-minute session

Mastery Objective

Students will be able to make connections when observing and discussing two works of art.

Essential Question

Why would we want to make connections between works of art?

Preassessment: Ask the students, "What connections can be made between two pieces of artwork?" and "How are the artworks alike or similar?"
Model (Think-Aloud):

- Using two pieces of artwork, model how you would make connections between two pieces of artwork. Refer to the elements of art (i.e., line, color, shape, texture, form, space, and value) and principles of design (i.e., pattern, repetition, contrast, balance, rhythm, movement, unity, and emphasis) when talking about the artwork. Use a large Venn diagram to record the similarities and differences.
- Show the class two more pieces of art and, as a whole group, have them discuss the similarities and differences of the two pieces using the elements and principles of art. Record their answers on a separate Venn diagram.

Group Work:

- Divide the class into groups of two.
- Hand each group a Venn diagram capture sheet (see page 26) and two smaller reproductions of artwork. (Consider providing some duplicate artworks to see whether different groups come up with the same answers.)
- Give the students fifteen minutes to work in groups and complete the diagram.
- Pull the class back together. Have groups share the important aspects of their work of art and give evidence for their answers.

Session 2: Connecting Art to Self

Time Frame

Two thirty-minute sessions (or one sixty-minute session)

Mastery Objective

Students will be able to make connections between themselves and the artworks of others.

Essential Question

Why would we want to make connections between our own lives and the artworks of others?

Preassessment: Ask the students, "What connections do artists make to their artwork?"
Model (Think-Aloud):

- Explain that an art to self connection is when you think about how the piece of art or story relates to you.
- Using a piece of artwork, model how you would make connections from yourself to the artwork. (e.g., "This reminds me of when I took a trip to the beach.")
- Ask the students the following questions:
  ◦ What does this painting remind you of?
  ◦ What experiences in your own life seem similar to this artwork?
  ◦ Do you have any other personal connections to this work of art?
- Show the class another painting, and as a whole group, have them make personal connections to the artwork using the guiding questions.

Group Work:

- Divide the class into groups of two.
- Hand each group a capture sheet and a calendar-size work of art.
- Give the students fifteen minutes to work in groups and complete the *Art to Self* capture sheet (see page 27).
- Pull the class back together. Have groups share the important aspects of their work of art and give evidence to support their answers.

Demonstration:

- Demonstrate how to create an observational drawing.
- Tell students that this is when an artist examines an object and draws what he or she really sees.

- Show students how to choose a natural object they have a connection with. (*Note*: Children can easily make connections to natural objects because it can remind them of places they have been or things they have done.)
- Show students how to draw the contour (inner and outer edges) of the object. Start slowly, and constantly look back and forth from your paper to the object. Follow the contour line of the object all the way around it. Then show students how to find lines in their object and fill in the inside. Make sure your demonstration drawing is very large, and encourage them to do the same.

Independent Work:

- Have students choose an object from the natural world. Have them tell a partner what connection they have to that natural object. Does it remind them of somewhere they have been? Or something they have done?
- Encourage the students to add a lot of details using lines; they can add color if there is time.

Session 3: Connecting Art to World

Time Frame

One thirty-minute session

Mastery Objective

Students will be able to make connections between artworks and the world around them.

Essential Question

Why would we want to make connections between artworks and the world around us?

Preassessment: Ask the students, "What connections do artists make in their artwork to their world?"

Model (Think-Aloud):

- Have the students help you list various world issues on a chart (e.g., global warming, rising gas prices, elections, homelessness, natural disasters).
- Display three to five works of art.
- Model how you would connect those world issues to works of art.
- Show the class other works of art, and as a whole group, ask them to make connections from the artwork to world issues.

Group Work:

- Place students in groups of two.
- Give students many pieces of artwork to share at their table. (Tip: Fill containers with art postcards or art-print magazines cut up into small pieces, and laminate them. These will be useful for a lot of different types of lessons.)
- Have students look through the group of artworks and make connections between world issues and the artwork.
- Ask pairs of students to complete the *Art to World* capture sheet on page 28.
- Bring the class back together and have students share their findings. Add more world issues to the list as needed.

Session 4: Culminating Art Experience

Time Frame

One sixty-minute session

Preassessment: Ask students to name and describe the different types of connections that have been previously discussed (post these: art to art, art to self, art to world).
Model (Think-Aloud):

- Think aloud as you brainstorm a list of possible connections to illustrate.
- Choose one and model how to sketch out a plan lightly with pencil.
- Demonstrate how to use colored pencils, oil pastels, markers, or crayons to add color to the picture.

Independent Work:

- Pass out 9-inch × 12-inch white paper, markers, pencils, crayons, and colored pencils.
- Ask the students to create a work of art that makes a connection to another work of art, themselves, or their world.
- Have students write the connection they made on the back of their finished artwork.

Closure: Allow time for students to share with the whole class or at their table groups.

TEACHING THE MAKING CONNECTIONS STRATEGY THROUGH READING/LANGUAGE ARTS

This reading/language arts lesson uses poetry. However, teachers may substitute picture books if they choose to do so.

Common Core: College and Career Readiness Anchor Standards for Reading

The following reading anchor standards are addressed in the reading lessons in this chapter:

Key ideas and details:
- Standard 2: Determine central ideas or themes of a text and analyze their development; summarize the key supporting details and ideas.
- Standard 3: Analyze how and why individuals, events, and ideas develop and interact over the course of a text.

Craft and structure:
- Standard 4: Interpret words and phrases as they are used in a text, including determining technical, connotative, and figurative meanings, and analyze how specific word choices shape meaning or tone.

Integration of knowledge and ideas:
- Standard 9: Analyze how two or more texts address similar themes or topics in order to build knowledge or to compare the approaches the authors take.

Range of reading and level of text complexity:
- Standard 10: Read and comprehend complex literary and informational texts independently and proficiently.

National Reading Standards

The following reading content standards are addressed in the reading lessons in this chapter:

Standard 1: Students read a wide range of print and nonprint texts to build an understanding of texts, of themselves, and of the cultures of the United States and the world; to acquire new information; to respond to the needs and demands of society and the workplace; and for personal fulfillment. Among these texts are fiction and nonfiction, classic and contemporary works.

Standard 3: Students apply a wide range of strategies to comprehend, interpret, evaluate, and appreciate texts. They draw on their prior experience, their interactions with other readers and writers, their knowledge of word meaning and of other texts, their word identification strategies, and their understanding of textual features (e.g., sound-letter correspondence, sentence structure, context, graphics).

Standard 4: Students adjust their use of spoken, written, and visual language (e.g., conventions, style, vocabulary) to communicate effectively with a variety of audiences and for different purposes.

Standard 9: Multicultural understanding—Students develop an understanding of and respect for diversity in language use, patterns, and dialects across cultures, ethnic groups, geographic regions, and social roles.

Standard 11: Participating in Society—Students participate as knowledgeable, reflective, creative, and critical members of a variety of literacy communities.

Standard 12: Students use spoken, written, and visual language to accomplish their own purposes (e.g., for learning, enjoyment, persuasion, and the exchange of information).

Sessions 1 and 2: Text to Self Connections

Mastery Objectives

Students will use their background knowledge to make connections between their personal life and a poem to deepen comprehension.

Time Frame

Approximately two forty-five-minute sessions

Session 1—Model the strategy
Session 2—Children read a new piece and complete their "connections boards"

Essential Questions

- How does using your background knowledge help you understand what you read?
- How does making connections between what you know and what you read help you understand the poem?
- How does making connections between what you know and what you read help you to understand the poet's message?

Materials

- A poem (that you connect with as a teacher) to use when you model the strategy of making text to self connections with your students
- Poems on topics children can relate to (e.g., summer, pets, weather, family)
- Picture books
- Poster-size manila paper
- Pencils and crayons
- Rulers
- Scissors

Preassessment:

- Tell the students that today they will make connections between their background knowledge and a poem/story they will be reading.
- Ask students to think about the art lessons they just did, and have them name ways that viewers make connections with artwork.
- Point out that just as viewers think about what they know or have experienced to help them bring meaning to a piece of art, readers also activate their own background knowledge in order to bring deeper meaning to what they read.

Model:

- Read aloud a poem. (e.g., "The Mother's Song" from *Songs Are Thoughts: Poems of the Inuit*, by Maryclare Foa and Neil Philip).
- After reading, use a think-aloud to tell children about the connections you made to the poem. Reread a few lines of the poem, and tell the children what these lines made you think about and how that helps you as the reader understand the poem better.
- Use the poster "Making Connections" to record your connections (see page 29).
- Ask the children whether anyone has a self to text connection to the poem. Have the children explain their connection.

Independent Work:

- Read aloud another poem to the children.
- Have them use the "quick sketch" strategy to record their connections. (A "quick sketch" is rapidly drawing out ideas/observations without using great detail. See chapter 3 for a template.)
- Provide time for them to make a "connections board." Children will use construction paper to make pictures of their connections. They will glue their pictures to the "connections board" and write words or phrases about their connections. (See worksheet on page 30.)
- Provide time for group sharing. Let children share their boards and explain the connections they made to the story.

Closure: Ask, "How does making connections help you to understand the poem better?"

Sessions 3 and 4: Text to Text Connections

Mastery Objectives

Students will use what they learned from one text to make connections to another text in order to deepen comprehension.

Time Frame

Two forty-minute periods

    Session 3—Model the strategy
    Session 4—Children read a new piece and complete their Venn diagram

Essential Questions

- How does using what you learned from one poem help you to understand another poem (text to text connections)?
- How does making connections between poems help you to understand the author, the author's message, or the literary techniques better?

Materials

- Poems that your students can connect to by the same poet or on the same topic (e.g., summer, pets, weather, family, different cultures), poems that have a similar message, or poems that use the same literary techniques (e.g., alliteration, similes, metaphors)
- Picture books (if not using poetry)
- Poster-size manila paper
- Pencils and crayons
- Rulers
- Scissors

Preassessment:

- Ask students to recall their work with making connections in art.
- Ask, "What do you remember about making *text to self connections* during the art lessons, and what did you use to make the connections?"
- Ask them, "How does making connections between what you know and what you read help you understand the story?" Refer to the chart on page 31 for connection ideas.
- Next, have students recall the art session on *making connections between art and art*.
- Tell them that today they will be making connections between two poems and that these connections are called *text to text connections*.
- Ask, "What do you think we can learn about a writer by reading different pieces by the same author?" (if using the same author's work), or "What do you think we can learn from comparing two poems (text to text connections)?"

Model (Think-Aloud):
Session 3: Model the Strategy:

- Using two poems, model how you would make connections between two poems. Refer to the topic of the poem, the use of language in the poem, or the artist's literary techniques in the poem to make connections (e.g., similes, metaphors, alliterations, etc.). Use a large Venn diagram to record your similarities and differences.
- Read the class two more poems and as a whole group, have them discuss the similarities and differences between the two poems. Have them focus on the topics, message, or literary techniques the poets used. Record their answers on a separate Venn diagram.

Session 4: Apply the Strategy:

Note: For this session, you can continue with poetry or use two different picture books (by the same author or different authors). If you use picture books, you may want to read one book one day and the second book the next day and then have the children do the group work on day 2.

Group Work:

- Divide the class into groups of two.
- Hand each group a Venn diagram capture sheet and two poems or passages (see page 32). (If using stories, do this step after you have read the second story to the class.)
- Give the students twenty-five minutes to work in groups and complete the diagram.
- Pull the class back together. Have groups share the connections they made between the two poems or stories.

Closure: Ask, "How did making connections between the two poems/stories help you to understand the poems/stories or author?"

Session 5: Text to World Connections

Mastery Objective

Students will be able to make connections between what they read in texts and the world around them.

Time Frame

One forty-minute period

Essential Questions

- How does using what you learned from one poem help you to make connections to something that is happening in your community or the world?

- How does making connections between poems and events in your community or the world help you better understand world events?

Materials

- World issues list made during the art lesson
- Poems or stories that provide information about community/world issues
- "Making Connections: Text to World" recording sheet (page 33)

Preassessment:

- Ask students to remember their work on connections in art. Have them recall the art session on making connections between art and the world.
- Tell them that today they will be making connections between what they read and a community/world issue.
- Ask the students, "How can making connections between what you read and your community/world help you to better understand your world?"

Model (Think-Aloud):

- Refer to the brainstorm list made in art on various community/world issues.
- Read aloud a poem, passage, or picture book.
- Model how you would connect the ideas in the poem/book to the community/world issues from your brainstorm list.
- Use the questions on the "Making Connections: Text to World" sheet to show students how you made connections between what you read and the world.

Independent Practice:

- Read another poem/picture book to your students.
- Ask students to use the "Making Connections" sheet.
- Bring the class back together and have students share their findings. Add more world issues to the list as needed.

Closure: Ask, "How did making connections between the two poems/stories help you to understand the poems/stories or author?"

Assessment Ideas

Most of the assessment ideas for this chapter will be completed through observation and analysis of the students' brainstorming and writing.

Note the following:

- During discussions, are children able to explain their connections and tell how this helps them better understand the piece of art or text?
- Are children able to use the Venn diagram, questions, and T-charts to develop and explain their connections?
- During the course of the lessons in art and reading, do children begin to expand on their connections and develop connections that deepen understanding of the art and/or text?

RESOURCES

Abercrombie, Barbara. (1990). *Charlie Anderson*. New York: Aladdin Paperbacks.

Foa, M., and Philip, N. (Eds.). (1995). *Songs Are Thoughts: Poems of the Inuit*. New York: Orchard Books.

MacLachlan, Patricia, and Charest, Emily. (2010). *I Didn't Do It*. New York: Katherine Tegen.

Olaleye, Issac. (1995). *The Distant Talking Drum*. Honesdale, PA: Wordsong.

Pinkney, Jerry. (2006). *The Little Read Hen*. New York: Penguin Group.

Rampersaud, Louise Bonnett. (2006). *Bubble and Squeak*. Tarrytown, NY: Marshall Cavendish.

Thomas, Joyce Carol. (1993). *Brown Honey in Broomwheat Tea*. New York: Harper-Collins.

Poetry anthologies such as:

- Roessel, David, and Rampersad, Arnold. (2006). *Poetry for Young People: Langston Hughes*. New York: Sterling.
- Sage, Allison. (1998). *The Treasury of Children's Poetry*. London: Hutchinson Children's Books.
- Worth, Valerie. (1996). *All the Small Poems and Fourteen More*. New York: Farrar, Straus & Giroux, 1996.

LITERACY BENEFITS

Teaching the strategy of making connections:

- helps children to activate their own background knowledge and use what they know to connect to new information in art and text.
- provides children with a framework for increasing comprehension.

- provides children with graphic organizers to use before, during, and after reading (T-chart, Venn diagram).
- allows children the opportunity to explain their thinking.
- builds on the reader's background knowledge.

Using art to teach how to make connections:

- builds confidence in children because most children have something to say about a piece of art.
- allows children the opportunity to apply the strategy in a text-free environment.
- creates a culture of learning by allowing all students to share their thinking based on artwork.
- provides students with the opportunity to apply and use art vocabulary when discussing works of art.

REFLECTION

Using art to teach how to make connections can help children learn the strategy in an environment that encourages risk taking. Many children do not feel threatened when responding to pictures. Their minds are freed up when they have to respond to a piece of art instead of make sense out of printed words. They are more likely to activate their own background knowledge, make connections between two prints or pieces by the same artist, and express how the painting is like something they know about in their community or world when using art. Explicitly teaching how to make connections in art first helps children understand this strategy. This makes them more likely to make connections when comprehending text after they have been successful with the strategy when applying it to artwork.

There are a number of reflections on our experience with the making connections lessons:

- Children enjoyed constructing their connection boards in the reading lessons. Letting them use art to make pictures of their connections gave visual and kinesthetic learners an opportunity to show their thinking in a different way.
- Students enjoyed sharing the connections they made with their classmates.
- Students developed freedom of thought and intellectual curiosity as they responded to a piece of artwork.
- Children deepened their understanding of works of art and poetry as they heard ideas from the teacher and their classmates.

- Children developed confidence in making connections and became better at identifying connections that deepened their understanding and connections that did not bring deeper meaning to the text or artwork.
- This lesson could also address the following two national standards by incorporating artwork that represents different cultures. Teachers can choose examples by artists from different cultures or backgrounds or artwork that depicts different cultural backgrounds.
  - Art content standard 4: Understanding the visual arts in relation to history and cultures
  - Reading standard 9: Students develop an understanding of and respect for diversity in language use, patterns, and dialects across cultures, ethnic groups, geographic regions, and social roles.

🎨 🎨 🎨 🎨 🎨 🎨 🎨 🎨 🎨 🎨 🎨 🎨 🎨

Making Connections: Art to Art

Name: _____ Teacher: _____

Directions: Using two pieces of artwork, fill out the similarities and differences on the diagram below.

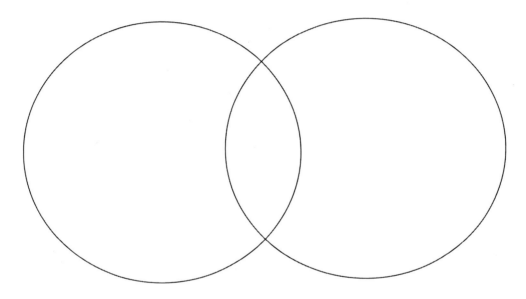

🎨 🎨 🎨 🎨 🎨 🎨 🎨 🎨 🎨 🎨 🎨 🎨

Making Connections: Art to Self

Name: _____ Teacher: _____

Directions: With a partner answer the following questions.

1. What does this painting remind you of?

2. What experiences in your own life seem similar to this artwork?

3. Do you have any other personal connections to this work of art?

Making Connections: Art to World

Name: _____ Teacher: _____

Directions: With a partner answer the following questions.

1. What art did you choose?

2. What is the world issue it relates to?

3. How does it relate?

Making Connections: Text to Self

Name: _____ Date: _____

Book Title: _____

Text Idea or Passage	Connection

Connections Board

Name: _____ Date: _____

Write or draw your connections below.

Making Connections

Name: _____ Date: _____

What do you connect with in this story or piece of artwork?

Art Connections	Story/Poem Connections
Topic/Subject	Main Idea/Theme
People	Characters
Mood/Color/Pattern	Setting
Story	Problem/Solution
Artist's Message	Writer's Message

🎨 🎨 🎨 🎨 🎨 🎨 🎨 🎨 🎨 🎨 🎨 🎨 🎨

Text to Text Connections

Name: _____ Date: _____

Directions: Using two picture books (or passages, poems, etc.), fill out the similarities and differences on the diagram below.

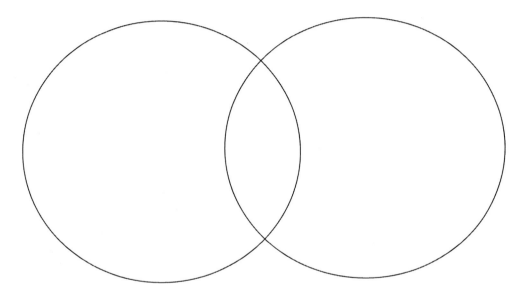

🎨 🎨 🎨 🎨 🎨 🎨 🎨 🎨 🎨 🎨 🎨 🎨 🎨

Making Connections: Text to World

Name: _____ Teacher: _____

Directions: With a partner answer the following questions.

1. What poem/story did you read?

2. What community/world issue does it relate to?

3. How does it relate?

QUESTIONING

Generating *Wonders*

Asking questions is part of remaining open to wonder and alert to the world around you.

> *7 Keys to Comprehension*
> (Zimmermann & Hutchins, 2003, p. 74)

Questions lead readers deeper into a piece, setting up a dialogue with the author, sparking in readers' minds what it is they care about.

> *7 Keys to Comprehension*
> (Zimmermann & Hutchins, 2003, p. 73)

Asking questions engages us and keeps us reading.

> *Strategies That Work*
> (Harvey & Goudvis, 2007, p. 109)

Asking questions before, during, and after reading is an important strategy that engages children in reading and deepens comprehension. According to Keene and Zimmermann (2007, pp. 135–36), readers ask questions for multiple purposes, including clarifying meaning, and understand how the process is used throughout their lives, academic and personal. The questions that readers ask about a text (e.g., questions about characters, settings, problems, solutions, themes) are what sparks thinking in readers and motivates them to read to find out answers to what they *wonder* about. Once children set their reason for reading through their questions, they need to decide whether:

- the text answers their questions;
- they need to use information in the text to infer their answers; or
- they need to do further research to answer their questions.

As with many of the comprehension strategies, some students are able to use this strategy easily, while other children might need help in understanding and applying this strategy. Children are generally very curious about the world around them and love to generate their own "wonder" questions. This can be an advantage to teaching the strategy. Building on children's love for asking questions and modeling how you, as an adult reader, ask questions before, during, and after reading will help children see how they can generate questions about what they read, what they see in works of art, and what they see in the world around them.

Some children need guidance as they work through the process with teacher modeling and support. Teaching children how to generate their own questions can be done through reading texts, stopping at key points, and giving the children an opportunity to ask questions. Then praise students for the questions they have that come from within them, the deeper-level, thick questions that are not answered from the text versus the thin questions that are easily answered from the text or are not relevant to the story.

In many classrooms, teachers are the ones who develop the questions for students most of the time. This may be one of the reasons some children have difficulty generating questions on their own. However, children need to develop this skill in order to be lifelong readers. What motivates one child may be different from what motivates another child. Children need to be encouraged to ask the questions that they wonder about, for it is this kind of wonder that will develop active readers and provide children with the lifelong skill of reading.

Teaching this strategy lets kids know that they have the power to tap into their own mind and generate questions that they truly care about, questions that can lead them deeper into the text, questions that spark their curiosity, and questions that lead them to further research, which can be very motivating for children.

Why Questioning?

Questioning is a necessary skill for developing thinking, setting purposes for reading, comprehending text, and understanding the world around you.

Questioning:

- motivates children to read as they search for the answers to their own questions;
- allows children to set purposes for reading;
- activates background knowledge;

- sparks interest;
- helps the reader focus;
- deepens comprehension;
- develops active readers; and
- develops higher-order thinking skills.

Why Art and Questioning?

The use of questioning allows students to immerse themselves in a book or a work of art. When students create deeper-level questions about a work of art, they are able to understand where the artist was coming from and start to make sense of the artwork's meaning. There is no text involved in the artwork that students will need to analyze (except perhaps the title of the work, which may be a clue toward its meaning), so students are able to use questions to begin to make their own meaning. It is widely accepted in the field of art to develop your own meaning while looking at artwork or that one piece of artwork may have several different interpretations. That is what makes looking at artwork so fun and exciting—the answers and possibilities are endless. The ability to have rich discussions with children where there is no right or wrong answer allows children to have the confidence to speak about whatever is on their mind. These are the deep conversations we want them to continue throughout their lifetime.

TEACHING THE QUESTIONING STRATEGY THROUGH ART

National Visual Arts Standards

The following art content standards are covered in the art lessons in this chapter:

Content standard 1: Understanding and applying media, techniques, and processes

Content standard 3: Choosing and evaluating a range of subject matter, symbols, and ideas

Content standard 5: Reflecting on and assessing the characteristics and merits of their work and the work of others

Content standard 6: Making connections between visual arts and other disciplines

Mastery Objectives

Students will be able to create and apply questioning strategies to explore works of art.
Students will create a work of art that depicts a past or future event in their lives.

Time Frame

Two to three forty-five- to sixty-minute sessions

Essential Question

How can the creation of deeper-level questions (thick questions) help viewers understand a work of art?

Art Vocabulary

> *Elements of art*: line, color, shape, texture, form, space, and value
> *Color families*: colors that are in specific groups
>> ° Primary colors: red, yellow, and blue
>> ° Secondary colors: orange, green, and purple
>> ° Cool colors: blues, greens, and purples
>> ° Warm colors: reds, oranges, and yellows
>> ° Complementary colors: colors that are across from each other on the color wheel. When placed next to each other in a work of art, these colors complement one another and add emphasis.
>
> *Mood*: a particular state of mind or feeling
> *Principles of design*: pattern, repetition, contrast, balance, rhythm, movement, unity, and emphasis

Materials

- Large reproductions of artwork (see "Resources" for suggestions)
- Large sticky notes
- T-chart
- Markers
- Premade questions that will be used to categorize the two types of questions
- 9-inch × 12-inch white drawing paper
- Various drawing materials such as pencils, erasers, crayons, markers, colored pencils, oil pastels

Session 1: Introduction of the Questioning Strategy

Before the students arrive:

- Choose two works of art for the preassessment. If you previously taught the making connections lessons, the artworks could be the same pieces so that the children are already familiar with them. Create four to six questions that clearly relate specifically to one or the other work of art.

- Choose an art reproduction, and cover a major portion of it with large sticky notes. Surrealist painters work really well for this lesson because their work typically evokes a lot of questions.
- Create a T-chart and label one side "Thick" and one side "Thin." Then cover the labels.
- Create six sample questions—three that are "thin" questions (easily answered by looking at the painting) and three that are "thick" questions (deep questions that require background information or the artist to answer).

See figure 2.1 for examples of "thick" and "thin" questions for art.

Preassessment:

- Display two pieces of artwork.
- Take out the premade questions you created about each piece, and give students the opportunity to match the questions to the appropriate art piece.
- Ask: "How will asking and answering questions help you better understand a work of art?"

Making Predictions Activity:

- Display the covered work of art.
- Ask students to make predictions about what is underneath.
- After a few predictions are verbalized, remove one sticky note.
- Continue this process of making predictions and removing sticky notes until the artwork is uncovered.

Questioning Activity:

- Using the T-chart, read two questions (one thin and one thick) and put them in the appropriate column on the T-chart. Ask students to categorize the remaining four questions.

Thin	Thick
1. What color is the sky in this painting? 2. What is the little girl holding in her hand? 3. What shapes do you see?	1. Where is the floating object in the center of the painting going? 2. Why is there a train coming out of the fireplace? 3. Why is the woman lying in the grass?

Figure 2.1. Examples of Thick and Thin Questions for Art (T-chart). These examples are from various artworks. For a list of possible artworks, see page 40.

- Ask students to predict what the name of each category is labeled. Reveal the answers.
- Ask students to work in groups to create more "thick" and "thin" questions on paper or sticky notes.
- Have other groups test their skills to see whether they can figure out which category the questions go in on the T-chart.

Conclusion: Ask the students, "Why did we create deeper-level questions (thick questions)? How did it help us better understand a work of art?"

Sessions 2–3: Past or Future Art Assignment

Preassessment/Review: Ask students to discuss the types of questioning skills they learned about in the last session.

Demonstration:

- Show students how to brainstorm a list of ideas for an artwork about either a past event in their lives or a future event they hope to experience.
- Model how to choose one event, and draw an outline of that on a piece of 9-inch × 12-inch white paper.
- Discuss various ways color can be added to the drawing (e.g., markers, colored pencils, crayons, oil pastels.).

Independent Work: Hand out paper and allow students to begin their drawings.

Closing Activity:

- Pair students and ask them to exchange artwork.
- Have pairs take turns asking each other thick questions.
- Summarize with the whole class by asking, "How can asking deeper-level questions (thick questions) help viewers understand a work of art?"

Artwork

- Homer, Winslow. *Breezing Up (A Fair Wind)*, 1873–1876
- Kaufman, Dana. *Self-Portrait*, 2003
- Magritte, René. *Voice of Space (La Voix des airs)*, 1931
- Magritte, René. *Time Transfixed (La Durée poignardée)*, 1938
- O'Keeffe, Georgia. *Jack-in-the-Pulpit No. IV*, 1930
- Rousseau, Henri. *Tiger in a Tropical Storm (Surprised!)*, 1891
- Wyeth, Andrew. *Christina's World*, 1948

TEACHING THE QUESTIONING STRATEGY THROUGH READING/LANGUAGE ARTS

Common Core: College and Career Readiness Anchor Standards for Reading

The following reading anchor standards are addressed in the reading lessons in this chapter:

Key ideas and details:
- ° Standard 1: Read closely to determine what the text says explicitly and to make logical inferences from it; cite specific textual evidence when writing or speaking to support conclusions drawn from the text.
- ° Standard 2: Determine central ideas or themes of a text and analyze their development; summarize the key supporting details and ideas.

Craft and structure:
- ° Standard 4: Interpret words and phrases as they are used in a text, including determining technical, connotative, and figurative meanings, and analyze how specific word choices shape meaning or tone.

Range of reading and level of text complexity:
- ° Standard 10: Read and comprehend complex literary and informational texts independently and proficiently.

National Reading Standards

The following reading content standards are addressed in the reading lessons in this chapter:

Standard 1: Students read a wide range of print and nonprint texts to build an understanding of texts, of themselves, and of the cultures of the United States and the world; to acquire new information; to respond to the needs and demands of society and the workplace; and for personal fulfillment. Among these texts are fiction and nonfiction, classic and contemporary works.

Standard 3: Students apply a wide range of strategies to comprehend, interpret, evaluate, and appreciate texts. They draw on their prior experience, their interactions with other readers and writers, their knowledge of word meaning and of other texts, their word identification strategies, and their understanding of textual features (e.g., sound-letter correspondence, sentence structure, context, graphics).

Standard 4: Students adjust their use of spoken, written, and visual language (e.g., conventions, style, vocabulary) to communicate effectively with a variety of audiences and for different purposes.

Standard 7: Students conduct research on issues and interests by generating ideas and questions and by posing problems. They gather, evaluate, and synthesize data from a variety of sources (e.g., print and nonprint texts, artifacts, people) to communicate their discoveries in ways that suit their purpose and audience.

Standard 11: Students participate as knowledgeable, reflective, creative, and critical members of a variety of literacy communities.

Mastery Objectives

- Students will be able to generate questions before, during, and after reading that lead to a deeper understanding of the text.
- Students will be able to categorize "thick" and "thin" questions for the story.

Time Frame

One one-hour session

Materials

- Two stories to be used as read-alouds—one for modeling and one for guided practice
- Sticky notes
- T-chart for "thick" and "thin" questions

Essential Questions

- How does asking deeper-level questions (thick questions) help readers understand a story?
- Why do readers ask questions before, during, and after reading?

Warm-up:

- Ask students to recall what they learned about questioning in the art lesson. Refer to the "thick and thin" question chart that they used with the painting. Take time to review the differences between "thick" questions (questions that make you wonder or questions that you may need to do research on to find the answers) and "thin" questions (questions that help you clear up confusions or questions that are easily answered by looking back at the text).
- Tell students that today, they will be applying the strategy to reading.

Teacher Modeling:

- Choose a good read-aloud story to model how to ask questions before, during, and after reading. (*Georgia's Bones* by Jen Bryant is a good text to use. This story ties art and reading together because it is about an artist. Many children enjoy reading stories about artists, and using books about artists may reinforce the connections children are making between learning a strategy in art and applying it to reading.)
- During the read-aloud, conduct a think-aloud. Stop at key points throughout the story to model how you are asking questions about the character and her actions. Modeling for children how you ask questions will help them to see how to ask questions themselves while reading. Write your questions down on sticky notes or use the chart on page 46. You can either prepare your questions ahead of time or ask a colleague to chart your questions on sticky notes while you are reading and modeling the strategy. Have "thick" and "thin" questions ready to share with the students. See figure 2.2 for examples of "thick" and "thin" questions for reading.
- After reading, have students help you to sort the questions on the "Thick" and "Thin" columns of the T-chart. Have children explain their thinking as to whether your question was a thick or thin question. Remind the children that thick questions are questions that make the reader wonder about something. After the children explain their thinking, share your thinking with the children, and build the T-chart together.

Guided Practice:

- Tell the children that today they will be generating their own questions about another story (e.g., *All I See* by Cynthia Rylant).Have them record their questions on the T-chart. Tell them that they may have a couple of "thin" questions, but that you would like them to focus on writing "thick" questions.
- After reading the title of the book, ask students to record one question they have about the book.

Thin	Thick
1. I wonder why she has a ribbon in her hair. 2. Why did she put the bones in a barrel? 3. Why did her mother make donuts?	1. I wonder why it is called *Georgia's Bones.* 2. I wonder why she collects things from nature. 3. Why did she keep seashells in her drawer? 4. I wonder why she liked shapes so much. 5. Why did she want to be an artist?

Figure 2.2. Examples of Thick and Thin Questions for Reading (T-chart).

- While reading the story, stop about halfway through and ask the students to record another question on their T-chart.
- After you finish the story, ask them to create at least one more question.
- Now that the story is finished, see whether students can go back and answer any of their questions.
- Provide them with the opportunity to identify their questions as "thick" or "thin."
- Remind them that the answers to "thin" questions are very evident, while the answers to "thick" questions can be debated—we might not all agree on the answer.
- Next, have the children work with partners to see whether they agree or disagree with how their partner classified their questions.
- Ask the children to share their questions with the group. Encourage them to label what kinds of questions they are (thin or thick) and explain their thinking.

Closure: Ask the students, "Why did we ask 'thick' questions about the story?" "How did it help you better understand the story?" and "Why do readers ask questions while they are reading?"

RESOURCES

Abercrombie, B. (1990). *Charlie Anderson*. New York: Aladdin Paperbacks.
Bryant, J. (2005). *Georgia's Bones*. Grand Rapids, MI: Eerdmans Books for Young Readers.
Raczka, B. (2002). *No One Saw—Ordinary Things through the Eyes of an Artist*. Minneapolis, MN: Millbrook Press.
Rylant, C. (1988). *All I See*. New York: Orchard Books.

LITERACY BENEFITS

The lessons in this chapter:

- require children to think as they determine whether their questions are "thick" or "thin" questions;
- provide time for children to express their thoughts and ideas when speaking or writing;
- require children to examine the artwork or text carefully in order to develop questions;
- allow children to cite evidence from the artwork or text to support their answers if the text or piece of artwork answers their questions;

- develop confidence in reluctant readers as they learn they have the power to ask questions;
- create a culture of learning by allowing all students to share their thinking based on the artwork or text, and also reflect on their classmates' answers; and
- provide students with the opportunity to apply and use art vocabulary when discussing works of art (elements of art and principles of design: color, line, shape, value, form, texture, space, pattern, repetition, contrast, balance, rhythm, movement, unity, and emphasis.).

REFLECTION

Using art to teach questioning can help build successful reading strategies for students. There are a number of reflections on our experience with the questioning lessons.

- Students were excited when they walked in the room and part of a painting was covered up. It was very mysterious and motivating.
- Students loved making predictions about what could be under the covered area. Uncovering each section at a time allowed students to refine their guesses.
- Using surrealist art was very different for students. It naturally creates lots of questions by all viewers.
- Students developed freedom of thought and intellectual curiosity as they created their own questions.
- Students developed the strategy of asking their own questions in order to comprehend art and text.

Questioning

Name: _____ Date: _____

Directions: While reading the text, record your questions you have about the story.

Book Title: _____

Thick Questions		
Page Number	**Question**	

VISUALIZING

Creating Pictures in Your Mind

Understanding, attending to, and developing a personal awareness of the sensory and emotional images that arise from reading give students the flexibility and capacity to experience an added depth of interpretation. It allows a passionate individual response and makes the text memorable by anchoring it to personal experience.

Mosaic of Thought (Keene & Zimmermann, 2007, p. 195)

Visualizing is one strategy used to create sensory images. Good readers use sensory impressions to gather information from the text that relates to their own backgrounds in order to understand what they read. Readers draw from all five senses and their own background knowledge to connect to text. In order to help students use sensory information, it is important to teach children to develop pictures in their mind. This is important, particularly for children who do not automatically use this strategy.

There are a number of ways to provide children with the opportunity to apply the strategy. For example, children can:

- create pictures from descriptions of artwork;
- create pictures after reading or listening to text; or
- illustrate their visualizations while listening to descriptions.

These lessons explicitly teach the strategy of visualizing through art first and then through reading.

Why Visualizing?

When you ask children to visualize, it:

- engages students in the text and makes it personal and memorable;
- develops active readers;
- allows for comprehension checkpoints while reading;
- permits children to share their visual images with other students in the classroom;
- permits students to make shifts in their thinking;
- elicits memories and feelings of the reader;
- deepens comprehension; and
- makes reading dynamic and exciting.

Why Art and Visualizing?

Keene and Zimmermann as well as other experts in education note that many children do not automatically use visualizing as a reading strategy. The goal of these lessons is to help students learn what it means to visualize and how to apply the strategy to artwork and text. In the following lessons, students learn to visualize in art and then apply the strategy to reading. They first create their own artwork while listening to a description of a piece of art. Breaking down the description of artwork into smaller chunks allows children to develop images in pieces. This provides a scaffold for helping children internalize the strategy.

At its core, art is visual and can be a valuable tool when linked with reading strategies. One reason children tend to find art less threatening than text is that there is no "right" or "wrong" answer when describing a work of art. Art provides a text-free environment, which helps students be risk takers. Children adjust their own thinking based on others' interpretations of artwork. Additionally, artwork naturally provokes memories as children connect to colors, moods, subject matter, facial expressions, and actions.

TEACHING THE VISUALIZING STRATEGY THROUGH ART

National Visual Arts Standards

The following art content standards are addressed in the art lessons in this chapter:

Content standard 1: Understanding and applying media, techniques, and processes
Content standard 3: Choosing and evaluating a range of subject matter, symbols, and ideas

Content standard 5: Reflecting upon and assessing the characteristics and merits of their work and the work of others

Content standard 6: Making connections between visual arts and other disciplines

Mastery Objectives

Students will work with partners to verbally describe a work of art while their partner visualizes a mental picture and then draws it.

Time Frame

One forty-five-minute session

Essential Question

How can creating visual images in our minds help us to better understand a work of art?

Art Vocabulary

- *Elements of art*: line, color, shape, texture, form, space, and value
- *Principles of design*: pattern, repetition, contrast, balance, rhythm, movement, unity, and emphasis
- *Quick sketch*: rapidly drawing out ideas/observations without great detail

Materials

- Large reproduction of artwork for modeling activity
- Chart paper for teacher modeling
- Quick Sketch template (page 57)
- Sets of two different prints for each pair (labeled print no. 1 and print no. 2)
- Manila folders (to stand up and block the partner's view)
- Thirty plastic chips (see "Teacher Note")
- Pencils, crayons, paper, erasers
- Elements of art and principles of design vocabulary chart

Teacher Note

Question chips: To limit the number of questions each student can ask his or her partner, give each child three plastic chips to "purchase" the answers to clarifying questions. Once the chips are used, the student can no longer ask questions. This encourages students to ask more thoughtful questions.

Introduction of the Strategy

Warm-up/Preassessment:

- Ask students to visualize a past event in their lives. Ask students to think about what the event looked like and to draw a picture of that event.
- Invite students to describe the process of creating their drawings. How did they decide what to draw and in what order?

Model/Demonstrate (Think-Aloud):
Note: You will need two teachers to model this activity.

- Introduce a quick sketch drawing and model this for the children. They will use this drawing technique this session. With a quick sketch, students rapidly draw out their ideas on paper, usually without great detail. With this technique, children record their ideas in drawing versus writing, freeing them to attend to the text without worrying about written expression and language mechanics.
- Show the class a print and let students look at it. Teacher A describes the print to teacher B. (Teacher B will not have seen the print.) When modeling this for students, use the elements of art and principles of design to describe the print.
- After teacher A describes the print, teacher B will visualize the print and record his or her thinking using a quick sketch. Emphasize that teacher B is recording on paper what he or she sees in his or her mind.
- Next, teacher B will compare the quick sketch to the original print.
- Let children know that they will be participating in a similar activity with a partner.

Group Work:

- Give each pair of students two prints in envelopes, three plastic chips, and manila folders. Assign students as partner A and B. Ask partner A to hold the print behind a folder so that it is out of sight of partner B.
- Distribute the "Create a Quick Sketch" template (page 57).
- Ask partner A to look at the print and think about how he or she will describe the print to partner B. Allow time for partner A to describe the print. Partner B will visualize what the print may look like and create a quick sketch of his or her thinking. Encourage the person who is describing to use the elements of art and principles of design in the description.

- Remind students that they can use the plastic chips to "purchase" the answers to three clarifying questions.
- Ask partner B to compare the sketch to the original print.
- Switch roles. Ask partner B to describe print number two to partner A.

Closure/Sharing:

- Ask students to share the original piece of art and their drawings with the class.
- Guide students as they look for similarities and differences in their peers' artwork.

Assessment Ideas:

- Challenge students to write a statement about how their drawing looks similar to the original artwork.
- Record anecdotal notes as students describe the similarities and differences in their peers' artwork.

Resources/Suggested Artwork

Any art will work for this lesson, but choose artwork that is simple and not abstract. The following pieces work well:

- Cezanne, Paul. *Still Life with Apples*, 1893–1894
- Monet, Claude. *Madame Monet and her Son*, 1875
- Hokusai, Katsushika. *The Great Wave of Kanagawa*, c. 1829–1832
- Wyeth, Andrew. *Christina's World*, 1948
- Wyeth, Andrew. *Wind from the Sea*, 1948
- Van Gogh, Vincent. *Blossoming Almond Branch in a Glass*, c. 1888

TEACHING THE VISUALIZING STRATEGY THROUGH READING/LANGUAGE ARTS

Common Core: College and Career Readiness Anchor Standards for Reading

The following reading anchor standards are addressed in the reading lessons in this chapter:

Key ideas and details:
° Standard 1: Read closely to determine what the text says explicitly and to make logical inferences from it; cite specific textual evidence when writing or speaking to support conclusions drawn from the text.

    ◦ Standard 2: Determine central ideas or themes of a text and analyze their development; summarize the key supporting details and ideas.

Craft and structure:

    ◦ Standard 4: Interpret words and phrases as they are used in a text, including determining technical, connotative, and figurative meanings, and analyze how specific word choices shape meaning or tone.

    ◦ Standard 5: Analyze the structure of texts, including how specific sentences, paragraphs, and larger portions of the text (e.g., a section, chapter, scene, or stanza) relate to each other and the whole.

Range of reading and level of text complexity:

    ◦ Standard 10: Read and comprehend complex literary and informational texts independently and proficiently.

National Reading Standards

The following reading content standards are addressed in the reading lessons in this chapter:

Standard 1: Students read a wide range of print and nonprint texts to build an understanding of texts, of themselves, and of the cultures of the United States and the world; to acquire new information; to respond to the needs and demands of society and the workplace; and for personal fulfillment. Among these texts are fiction and nonfiction, classic and contemporary works.

Standard 4: Students adjust their use of spoken, written, and visual language (e.g., conventions, style, vocabulary) to communicate effectively with a variety of audiences and for different purposes.

Standard 11: Students participate as knowledgeable, reflective, creative, and critical members of a variety of literacy communities.

Mastery Objectives

Students will apply the strategy of visualizing by creating illustrations that depict the visual imagery they have in their minds while listening to a poem.

Time Frame

One forty-five-minute session

Essential Questions

- How does making pictures in your mind during reading help you understand the story?
- How can making pictures in your mind help you understand what the author/poet is describing?

Materials

- Descriptive phrases
- Three poems of different length/difficulty copied onto chart paper
- Paper for the students' illustrations
- Pencils, crayons, and erasers

Introduction of the Strategy

Warm-up/Preassessment:

- Ask the students whether they enjoy poetry. Ask them whether they make pictures in their minds while listening to poems.
- Tell them that today they are going to be listening to poems and making pictures in their minds.
- Explain how making pictures in your mind helps you connect to the poem and remember it better.

Model/Demonstrate (Think-Aloud):

- Read a few descriptive phrases aloud.
- Think aloud (explain your thinking) about what pictures come to your mind while reading the phrases. Point out what you already know about the phrases. For example, if the phrase was, "The flowers were bending in the wind," tell the children how you have seen flowers bending in the wind and what that looked like to you.
- After you explain your connections to the students and what you are visualizing, use the quick sketch (page 57) method to model how to illustrate what you are visualizing in your mind. By modeling using the quick sketch method, you help students make the connection between using the strategy in art and reading. With a quick sketch, students rapidly draw out their ideas on paper, usually without great detail. Students record their ideas in drawing versus writing, freeing them to attend to the text without worrying about written expression and language mechanics.

CHAPTER 3

Guided Practice:

- Give the students a phrase and have them use the quick sketch technique to record their visual images.
- Allow students the opportunity to share their quick sketches with the group.

Independent Work:

- Read the three poems of different length/difficulty, copied onto chart paper, aloud to the children.
- Let the students choose the poem they want to visualize and illustrate.
- If possible, arrange to have two other adults in the room. Split the students into three different groups. Each adult should work with one group. Have the adults reread the poem. While children are listening to the second reading, ask them to close their eyes and listen to the poem. Encourage children to use the words from the poem to create pictures in their minds.
- The students will draw what they visualize in their minds.

Closure/Sharing:

- Post the drawings on the bulletin board. Facilitate a class vote to determine which illustrations go with each poem. Ask students to share what they were thinking while listening to the poem.
- Ask students how the strategy may help them better understand the poem and when they might use this strategy in reading.

Assessment Ideas:

- Challenge students to write a statement about how their illustration represents the visual images they had while listening to the poem.
- Observe and note whether students are able to illustrate the key ideas in a poem.

RESOURCES

Suggested descriptive phrases:

- The flowers were bending in the wind.
- The butterfly floats across the tops of the flowers.
- The snow blankets the flowers in white.

There are many poems that work for this lesson. Choose poems with descriptive language that students can easily visualize. Also, choose poems with varying degrees of difficulty that meet the needs of the students in your class. The following poetry resources are suggestions for instruction:

Foa, M., and Philip, N. (Eds). (1995). *Songs Are Thoughts—Poems of the Inuit*. New York: Orchard Books.

Hall, D. (Ed). (1999). *The Oxford Illustrated Book of American Children's Poems*. New York: Oxford University Press.

Huang, T. (1992). *In the Eyes of Cats*. New York: Henry Holt.

Olaleye, I. (1995). *The Distant Talking Drum—Poems from Nigeria*. Honesdale, PA: Wordsong.

Shannon, G. (1996). *Spring, A Haiku Story*. New York: Greenwillow Books.

Yolen, J. (2000). *Color Me a Rhyme*. Honesdale, PA: Wordsong.

LITERACY BENEFITS

- All students, including English language learners (ELL), will get the opportunity to use descriptive language to describe a painting to their partner.
- Children will have the experience of applying the visualizing strategy to the art and to reading.
- Children will be participating in text-free activities to learn more about the comprehension strategy of "visualizing."
- The quick sketch method can be used as a reference as they talk about the mental images they are creating.
- Children will have multiple opportunities to visualize and internalize the strategy in order to deepen their comprehension.

REFLECTION

- Visualization with art can be a powerful tool in developing new reading strategies for students. Providing opportunities for children to sketch their ideas allowed the teacher to see whether the children could apply the strategy. Using artwork first enables children to apply the strategy without text.
- Children enjoyed the teacher demonstrations. No matter how skilled you are as an artist, children enjoy seeing their teachers demonstrate the technique they will be using. Don't be surprised if you hear, "Wow, you are a good artist!"

- In the art lesson, students were very engaged while listening to their peers describe the master work of art and then drawing what they visualized during the description. The students compared this activity to a "guessing game."
- Students enjoyed looking at their peers' pictures displayed together and comparing their pictures to the master artist's work.

Create a Quick Sketch

Name: _____ Date: _____

Directions: Use the box here to create a quick sketch of the picture in your mind. Rapidly draw out your ideas below, without great detail.

INFERRING

Reading between the Lines

Inferring is the process of creating a personal and unique meaning from text. It involves a mental process that combines information gleaned from the text and relevant prior knowledge (schema).

Mosaic of Thought (Keene & Zimmermann, 2007, p. 166)

Inferring is part rational, part mystical, part definable, and part beyond definition.

Mosaic of Thought (Keene & Zimmermann, 2007, p. 145)

The strategy of inferring is a necessary skill so that readers can create a deeper, more personal understanding of the text. Many readers are good at interpreting text at the literal level but need support to learn how to infer. Inferring is also known as "reading between the lines"; through inferences, readers interpret the literal information, combine it with their own knowledge, and create meaning from the text.

There are similarities between making predictions and drawing inferences. A prediction can be a type of inference. According to Harvey and Goudvis (2007), we make predictions about events, outcomes, or actions in the story that are resolved after we finish reading the book. However, inferences may never be resolved.

As children continue to read, they revise their predictions based on information from the text. Making inferences is a personal journey the students take because they are drawing on their own unique background experiences.

CHAPTER 4

Why Inferring?

Inferring is a necessary skill for comprehending text and understanding the world around you. Inferring:

- engages students in text and allows them to use their background knowledge while reading,
- deepens comprehension,
- develops active readers, and
- develops higher-order thinking skills.

In addition, state testing requires children to infer in order to understand text passages and respond to test questions.

Why Art and Inferring?

There are many benefits to using art to teach the skill of inferring to children. First, because paintings are visual, children automatically need to make inferences in order to bring meaning to the piece of art. With a painting, children use the elements of art (color, form, shape, line, space, texture, and value) to interpret and discuss artwork. Children then apply their own knowledge (schema) about what they see in artwork to understand it. Children use their schema to develop a deeper meaning about the piece.

Using art, teachers can explicitly teach the skill of inferring. Art can act as a scaffold. By first applying the strategy to a "text-free" environment, children can develop an understanding of what inferring is without the demands of text. Artwork allows children to use the visual information given by the artist and then add their own knowledge to construct meaning. A goal of this approach is to have children be successful in applying the strategy in a text-free environment before moving to text. Once they can apply the strategy to art, children will be ready to move to text.

TEACHING THE INFERRING STRATEGY THROUGH ART

National Visual Arts Standards

The following art content standards are addressed in the art lessons in this chapter:

Content standard 1: Understanding and applying media, techniques, and processes
Content standard 3: Choosing and evaluating a range of subject matter, symbols, and ideas

Content standard 5: Reflecting on and assessing the characteristics and merits of their work and the work of others

Content standard 6: Making connections between visual arts and other disciplines

Mastery Objectives

Students will be able to make inferences when talking about works of art.

Students will use color and facial expressions to create mood in a work of art.

Time Frame

Four thirty- to forty-five-minute sessions

Essential Questions

- How do artists use color and facial expressions to tell the mood and the "story" in the painting?
- How does the strategy of inferring help us to understand a piece of art?

Art Vocabulary

Elements of art: line, color, shape, texture, form, space, and value

Collage: a composition or design made by arranging and gluing materials to a background surface

Cool colors: blues, greens, and purples

Mood: a particular state of mind or feeling

Pattern: a design created by repetition of symbols, motifs, lines, colors, and textures on the surfaces

Portrait: a pictorial representation of a person

Principles of design: pattern, repetition, contrast, balance, rhythm, movement, unity, and emphasis

Warm colors: reds, oranges, and yellows

Materials

- Large reproductions of artwork (see "Resources" for suggestions)
- Lined paper or inference worksheet
- Pencils
- Paper: precut 12-inch × 12-inch sheets

- Construction paper, assorted colors, 12-inch × 12-inch or 9-inch × 12-inch
- Pencils/erasers
- Examples of portraits that show different emotions
- Colored pencils
- Assorted mixed media materials (e.g., foil, tissue paper, cardboard, magazines, texture paper, or rubbings)
- Mirrors
- Individual whiteboards or chart paper and markers

Session 1: Introduction of the Strategy (Think, Pair, Share)

Preassessment: Ask the students to develop a working definition of "inferring" on individual whiteboards or a class poster.

Model (Think-Aloud):

- Display a work of art that depicts a narrative or mood.
- Demonstrate how to infer, using your background knowledge and visual clues from the artwork.
- Demonstrate how to think, pair, and share by giving the children individual think time, having the children work with a partner to verbalize their thinking, and then having partners share with the whole group.

Group Work:

- Display a different work of art that depicts narrative or mood.
- Have students select a partner.
- Have students think, pair, and share with their partner about the narrative or mood of the new piece of artwork.

Independent Work (Writing): Provide an opportunity for students to write down their inferences. (Use the inference template on page 71 and see possible sentence starters on page 72.)

Sharing: Students share their inferences with the class.

Closure:

- Have the students expand upon their working definition of inferring that they created at the beginning of the lesson.
- Guide students while they share their new definition with the class.
- Create a class definition of inferring.

Assessment Idea: Observe and record how students support their inferences with details from the artwork. Examples of student writing (spelling has not been changed):

I think they are poor because they have ragady clouse. I think they lost their baby in a storm and they tride to go to a worm place. And the backraund looks like it is cold. (second grader)

I thik with the thee polpel were travuling but there bot crash and to little pesis When it was morning then they wer on this ilalnt and they wer sad because they din't have any mony and nuthing to eat or were. (second grader)

Sessions 2–3: Art Experience (Emotion Collage)

Session 1: Sketching and Planning

Preassessment: Determine students' prior knowledge by asking:

- What is a portrait?
- Describe the difference between these two portraits.

Guided Discussion:

- Ask students to identify and compare selected portraits.
- Facilitate a discussion about different emotions and how artists portray those emotions. (Use the elements of art and principles of design in the discussion.)

Demonstration:

- Give each student a mirror and have students practice making emotions while looking in the mirror. Ask them to note what their facial features do when making a specific emotion. Have the students discuss their observations with the class.
- Demonstrate how to sketch a head, neck, and shoulders. Emphasize filling up the space on the paper.
- Explain and show students the proportions of the face. (See Betty Edwards, *Drawing on the Right Side of the Brain*, page 145.)
- Have students use the proportions practice sheet on page 73.
- Discuss how the emotion has to be clear in their portrait so that others will be able to infer their emotion easily.
- Model how to create emotion in their facial features, like raised eyebrows to show surprise or anger. Demonstrate ways that any feature (e.g., eyes, eyebrows, position of the head, mouth) can show emotion.

Independent Work: Distribute the paper and ask students to begin to draw their portraits with an emotion.

Formative Assessment: Assist students as they begin drawing their portraits.

Conclusion/Closure:

- Guide students as they clean up and put materials away.
- Exit question: What is the emotion you expressed in your drawing? What facial features did you use to express that emotion? (See the "Exit Card" on page 74.)

Sessions 2–3: Color Choice/Collage

Preassessment: Determine students' prior knowledge by asking:

- How can colors evoke a feeling?
- How does color affect your interpretation of the mood communicated in the portrait?
- What else can you do to create an emotion? What facial expressions can imply a feeling?

Guided Discussion: Guide students in a discussion about how color affects mood in portraits.

Demonstration:

- Show students how to pick the paper for their portraits. Remind students to think about the color/emotion in their compositions.
- Model how to tear the paper into small pieces and cover the face with a color.
- Demonstrate how to use the paper to create emotion in their eyes, nose, and mouth.
- Show how to add eyebrows with mixed media: paper, sandpaper, crayon rubbings, magazine paper, newspaper, tissue paper, and so on.
- Demonstrate how to use paper techniques to create hair (tear, fringe, roll, etc.).

Independent Work:

- Distribute student-created portraits.
- Display teacher examples of different options that could be used for their portraits.
- Ask students to begin using torn paper to create their emotion collages.

Formative Assessment: Assist students as they begin to create their paper collages. Provide feedback and offer suggestions.

Conclusion:

- Paper clip pieces of paper together and store.
- Exit question: Did you create an emotion or mood in your portrait? Write down your mood or emotion and describe how you created that emotion. Were you successful in creating a portrait that expresses an emotion or mood? How do you know?

Assessment Idea/Summative Activity—Gallery Walk:

- Display each student's work at his or her seat.
- Give the students pencils and five to ten index cards or sticky notes. Have the students write their names on the back of each index card or sticky note.
- Guide students as they walk around the room and look at the emotion collages.
- Encourage students to use clues from the collage to infer the emotion portrayed in the artwork.
- Have students write down the emotion on the card and lay the card upside down next to their peers' work so that other students cannot see their comments.
- Provide students with ten to fifteen minutes to do this part of the activity, and then have them return to their seats to look at what their peers wrote.
- Hold up some of the artwork and have the students share what clues they used to infer that emotion.

Resources

Books

Edwards, B. (2012). *Drawing on the Right Side of the Brain*. New York: Tarcher.

Venezia, M. (1988). *Getting to Know the Artist: Pablo Picasso*. Danbury, CT: Children's Press.

Venezia, M. (2004). *Getting to Know the Artist: Winslow Homer*. Danbury, CT: Children's Press.

Artworks

- Homer, Winslow. *The Fog Warning*, 1885
- Homer, Winslow. *The Gulf Stream*, 1899
- Picasso, Pablo. *The Tragedy*, 1901
- Picasso, Pablo. *Head*, 1960

TEACHING THE INFERRING STRATEGY THROUGH READING/LANGUAGE ARTS

Common Core: College and Career Readiness Anchor Standards for Reading

The following reading anchor standards are addressed in the reading lessons in this chapter:

Key ideas and details:
- ° Standard 1: Read closely to determine what the text says explicitly and to make logical inferences from it; cite specific textual evidence when writing or speaking to support conclusions drawn from the text.
- ° Standard 3: Analyze how and why individuals, events, and ideas develop and interact over the course of a text.

Craft and structure:
- ° Standard 4: Interpret words and phrases as they are used in a text, including determining technical, connotative, and figurative meanings, and analyze how specific word choices shape meaning or tone.

Range of reading and level of text complexity:
- ° Standard 10: Read and comprehend complex literary and informational texts independently and proficiently.

National Reading Standards

The following reading content standards are addressed in the reading lessons in this chapter:

Standard 1: Students read a wide range of print and nonprint texts to build an understanding of texts, of themselves, and of the cultures of the United States and the world; to acquire new information; to respond to the needs and demands of society and the workplace; and for personal fulfillment. Among these texts are fiction and nonfiction, classic and contemporary works.

Standard 3: Students apply a wide range of strategies to comprehend, interpret, evaluate, and appreciate texts. They draw on their prior experience, their interactions with other readers and writers, their knowledge of word meaning and of other texts, their word identification strategies, and their understanding of textual features (e.g., sound-letter correspondence, sentence structure, context, graphics).

Standard 4: Students adjust their use of spoken, written, and visual language (e.g., conventions, style, vocabulary) to communicate effectively with a variety of audiences and for different purposes.

Standard 11: Students participate as knowledgeable, reflective, creative, and critical members of a variety of literacy communities.

Mastery Objectives

Students will be able to make inferences while listening to a story.

Time Frame

One one-hour session

Essential Questions

- How does using the strategy of "inferring" help us understand a story?
- How can we use our schema to understand the story at a deeper level?

Materials

- Prints used from the art-inferring lesson
- Cartoon/wordless picture book to use for students to use to make inferences
- Simple action sentences to read to children to make inferences (see lesson plan)
- Text for teacher to read aloud and model (e.g., *See the Ocean* by Estelle Condra)
- Sticky notes
- "Inferring: Charting Your Responses" (see page 75)

Introduction of the Strategy

Warm-up:

- Display a cartoon or wordless picture book and ask the children to state what they see in the picture. Gather and chart responses. Then ask them what they think is happening in the cartoon.
- Next, display a few action sentences, such as,
    ○ "Before going to school, Alice put on her raincoat."
    ○ "When they heard the ice cream truck coming, the children went in to get their money."
- Ask the children to elaborate on what is happening in each sentence. Explain that when they are interpreting a cartoon or a wordless picture book, they are making inferences. Tell the class that they will be making inferences with stories as they did

when they made inferences in art using pictures. Remind the children of the art lessons and how they used inferring to understand the pictures.

Teacher Modeling:

- Choose a read-aloud story to model how you make inferences while you are reading (e.g., *See the Ocean* by Estelle Condra).
- During the read-aloud, conduct a "think-aloud." Stop at key points throughout the story to model how you are using information from the text and your prior knowledge to make inferences about the main character. Modeling how to make inferences will help make the strategy of inferring visible.
- As you think aloud, pause at key stopping points and use the template to model your thinking. (See possible sentence starters on page 72.) Consider making a poster-size chart to use for your modeling.

Teacher Note: You may find it helpful to use the chart on page 76 with students to help them understand that they have the power to infer. Some students are able to read the text or look at the piece of art but do not understand that they need to be interpreting what they are seeing. The chart is designed to help students realize that they have the power to think about the art/text and think about what they know regarding what the art/text is telling them in order to create meaning.

Guided Practice:

- After making the connection between your read-aloud and the inferring they did with artwork, tell the children that they will be making inferences while listening to a story.
- Distribute the "Charting Your Responses" or the "Use Your Power" sheet (pages 75 and 76) for students to record their thinking.
- Read aloud a story that requires students to make a lot of inferences, such as *The Table Where the Rich People Sit*, by Byrd Baylor and Peter Parnall, or *Tight Times*, by Barbara Shook Hazen.
- Stopping at key places in the text, ask the children to record their inferences and support for their thinking on the "Charting Your Responses" sheet.
  - Throughout the story, have some of the children share their thinking.
  - Listen to the responses, checking to make sure the children are using evidence from the text to make their inferences.
  - At the end of the story, ask the children to share their inferences and explain their thinking.
- Ask the students how inferring helps them understand the story better and how they will use the strategy while reading text.

Assessment Ideas:

- Observe whether children are able to share their inferences and explain their thinking.
- Note whether children are able to support their inferences with examples from the text.

Templates:

- Making Inferences Using Art: What Can You Infer? (page 71)
- Sentence Starters (page 72)
- Proportions Practice Sheet (page 73)
- Exit Cards (page 74)
- Inferring: Charting Your Responses (page 75)
- Use Your Power (page 76)

RESOURCES

Anno, M. (1978). *Anno's Journey*. Cleveland, OH: William Collins & World.

Baker, J. (2004). *Home*. New York: Greenwillow Books.

Bang, M. (1980). *The Grey Lady and the Strawberry Snatcher*. Cincinnati, OH: Four Winds Press.

Baylor, B., and Parnall, P. (1998). *The Table Where the Rich People Sit*. New York: Aladdin.

Condra, E. (1994). *See the Ocean*. Nashville, TN: Ideals.

DePaola, T. (1978). *Pancakes for Breakfast*. Troy, MO: Harcourt Brace Jovanovich.

Hazen, B. S. (1983). *Tight Times*. London: Puffin.

McCully, E. A. (2001). *Four Hungry Kittens*. New York: Penguin Putnam.

Tafuri, N. (1987). *Do Not Disturb*. New York: Greenwillow Books.

LITERACY BENEFITS

The lessons in this chapter:

- provide opportunities for children to make inferences in a text-free environment;
- create a deeper understanding of what is being read;
- build on what is known by the child;
- allow the opportunity for children to verbalize their thinking;

- create a culture of learning by allowing all students to share their thinking about the artwork or text;
- provide students with the opportunity to apply and use art vocabulary when discussing works of art;
- provide students with the opportunity to make inferences from peers' work.

REFLECTION

Using art to teach inferring can help build successful reading strategies for students. There are a number of reflections on our experience with the inferring lessons.

- Students enjoyed the opportunity to view, discuss, and interpret artwork.
- Students developed freedom of thought and intellectual curiosity as they used what the artist gave them to develop their own thinking.
- Children deepened their understanding that art and writing are forms of communication.
- Children deepened their understanding that they have the ability to comprehend art and text by bringing their own background knowledge to the piece.
- Students discovered that they have the power and maturity to interpret pieces of art and text.

Making Inferences Using Art

What Can You Infer?

Name: _____ Date: _____

Directions: Using the artwork posted, write your inferences in the space below.

_____
_____
_____
_____
_____
_____

What clues in the artwork or personal experiences make you think that?

_____
_____
_____
_____
_____
_____

Sentence Starters for Recording Inferences

When answering inference questions, teach children to begin their sentence using the following:

The artist showed _____.

I know _____.

I think _____because

_____.

For more advanced students, use the following:

- This makes me think . . .

- Maybe it means . . .

- I'm guessing that . . .

Proportions Practice Sheet

Name: _____ Date: _____

Directions: Use the oval below to practice the proportions of the face.

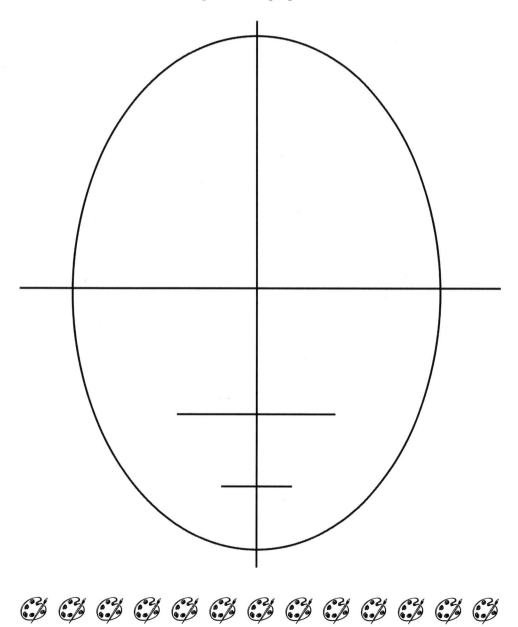

Name:_____Date:_____

Exit Question:
What is the emotion you expressed in your drawing?

_____

What facial features did you use to express that emotion?

_____
_____
_____
_____

Name:_____Date:_____

Exit Question:
What is the emotion you expressed in your drawing?

_____

What facial features did you use to express that emotion?

_____
_____
_____
_____

Inferring
Charting Your Responses

Name: _____ Date: _____

Text	What I Know...	I Can Infer...

Use Your Power!

Name: _____ Date: _____

What does the writer tell me?	What do I know?	I can infer . . .

DETERMINING IMPORTANCE

Selecting the Important Parts

The ability to identify essential ideas and salient information is prerequisite to developing insight.

Strategies That Work (Harvey & Goudvis, 2007, p. 156)

Readers of nonfiction have to decide and remember what is important in the texts they read if they are going to learn anything from them.

Strategies That Work (Harvey & Goudvis, 2007, p. 156)

What is important in nonfiction text? How do children know? What facts/information do children need to remember after reading? What is the essential information? In order to find the answers to these questions, children need to learn how to *determine what is important in the text* they read. They need to make decisions about what information they can let go of and what information they need to keep. How children determine what is essential before, during, and after reading has to do with:

- their purpose for reading;
- the questions they develop about the topic prior to reading;
- their background knowledge; and
- how children understand how writers use text features to organize information.

According to Harvey and Goudvis, readers need to "sift and sort the important information from the details and merge their thinking with it" (*Strategies That Work*, p. 176). Determining importance is a very important strategy for readers and can be challenging for some children. In order to help children determine what is important in nonfiction text, teachers need to be explicit when teaching children how to do this. One way to teach children to determine what is important in text is to show them what authors do to help readers sift through the information. Authors include text features to tell the reader, "Hey, look at me, this information is important!" Teaching children the purpose of text features will help them to see what the author thinks is important. Some of the text features used in the following lessons are:

- bold-print words;
- picture captions;
- headings;
- index;
- fact boxes;
- glossaries;
- pictures/photographs; and
- the table of contents.

Teaching children about these text features will help them identify the features in text and learn to gather information from the text features. Learning about text features will also help children understand how authors organize text and provide a framework for children to use when navigating nonfiction text.

Why Determining Importance?

Determining importance is a necessary skill for comprehending text and making decisions about what is important in text and the world around you. Learning how to determine importance in text:

- engages students in text;
- develops active readers;
- helps readers to locate answers to their questions;
- teaches children to distinguish between important information in text and interesting information;
- allows readers to use their background knowledge while reading;
- teaches children "the code" (text features) writers use to organize information in nonfiction text (table of contents, bold-print words, picture captions, headings, fact boxes, index, glossary, pictures, photographs); and
- empowers children to locate information in text.

In addition, state testing requires children to determine important main ideas, themes, and information from various reading passages. As Keene and Zimmerman (2007, *Mosaic of*

Thought, p. 219) point out, determining importance is also a skill we use throughout the day as we make decisions and judgments.

Why Art and Determining Importance?

There are many benefits to using art to teach the skill of determining importance to children. Art is a visual medium, and when children look at artwork they are not overwhelmed by text. When using art first to learn determining importance, children can focus on the "codes" that artists use to communicate ideas and meaning about their work. When children look at a piece of art, they have to comprehend what the artist is saying and draw meaning from the piece. For a viewer to be able to determine what is important in a work of art, he or she needs to be able to decipher the clues (elements of art and principles of design) the artist uses to communicate meaning. Some of those clues might include:

- focal point/emphasis;
- space (foreground, middle ground, background);
- color (bright vs. muted);
- movement;
- mood;
- style;
- line; and
- shape.

Once children understand the clues or codes that an artist uses, they can make connections to understand that an author also uses codes (text features) to help readers determine what is important.

TEACHING THE DETERMINING IMPORTANCE STRATEGY THROUGH ART

National Visual Arts Standards

The following art content standards are addressed in the art lessons in this chapter:

Content standard 1: Understanding and applying media, techniques, and processes

Content standard 2: Using knowledge of structures and functions

Content standard 3: Choosing and evaluating a range of subject matter, symbols, and ideas

Content standard 5: Reflecting on and assessing the characteristics and merits of their work and the work of others

Content standard 6: Making connections between visual arts and other disciplines

Mastery Objectives

Students will be able to determine what is important when looking at works of art.
Students will be able to use the elements of art and principles of design to create a work
  of art with a focal point.

Time Frame

Two to three forty-five- to fifty-minute sessions

Essential Question

How do artists communicate what is important in their artwork?

Art Vocabulary

Foreground: the part of the pictures that is represented nearest to the viewer
Middle ground: the space between the foreground and the background in the picture
  plane
Background: the parts of an artwork that seem to be farthest away
Emphasis: a principle of design that refers to a way of combining elements to stress the
  differences between those elements and to create one or more centers of interest in
  an artwork
Focal Point: the portion of an artwork's composition on which interest or attention
  centers
Detail: small parts that make up the whole

Artists/Artworks

There are lots of artworks that show emphasis and have a focal point. Choose artwork that
has a center of interest and a subject that will interest students. Some examples are:

- Cassatt, Mary. *The Boating Party*, 1893/1894
- Lawrence, Jacob. *Cabinet Maker*, 1957
- Matisse, Henri. *The King's Sadness*, 1952

Materials

- Two large reproductions of artwork (to be seen by the class)
- Fifteen to twenty smaller reproductions of artwork (to be seen by individual students
  or pairs)

- Capture sheet
- Pencils
- Watercolor paper
- Watercolors
- Watercolor paintbrushes
- Water containers
- Paper towels

Session 1: Introduction of the Strategy

Preassessment: Ask the students, "How do you determine what is important in a work of art?"

Model (Think-Aloud):

- Using a piece of artwork, model how you would determine the important parts. Use the art vocabulary words on page 80 to discuss the artwork.
- Discuss the difference between the foreground, middle ground, and background (see figure 5.1).
- Discuss how artists show emphasis by using bright colors, contrasting colors, and sizes.
- Show the class another painting and as a whole group, have them discuss what the most important parts of the painting are and why.
- Remind students to use the art vocabulary words when explaining their ideas.

Group Work:

- Provide pairs of students with a capture sheet (page 88) and smaller-size work of art. Consider providing some groups with the same images to see whether different groups come up with similar answers.
- Give the students fifteen minutes to work in groups and complete the capture sheet.
- Have groups share the important aspects of their work of art and give evidence for their answers.

Foreground	Middle ground	Background
Large objects The most detail Closest to the viewer More vibrant color Lowest on the picture plane (usually)	Medium-sized objects Some detail Center of the picture plane	Small objects Not much detail Far away from the viewer Muted colors Highest on the picture plane (usually)

Figure 5.1. Differences between foreground, middle ground, and background.

Independent Work: Give students the brainstorming worksheet (page 89) to help them develop ideas and sketches for their artwork.

Closure: Review the vocabulary for the day and tell the students that next time they will use watercolor to create paintings.

Sessions 2–3: Emphasis/Focal Point Painting

Preassessment:

- Display the smaller pictures showing emphasis and focal point from the last class.
- Have the students tell you what the most important part of the artwork is and how they know.

Demonstration:

- Show students how to transfer their sketches onto the watercolor paper. Demonstrate how to use lightly drawn lines so that the pencil does not show through the watercolor paint.
- Demonstrate how to use watercolor paint. Wet your brush first and then put the brush in the paint. Use the paper towel to soak up any excess water on your brush if you have too much.
- Show students how to use the tip of the brush to make smaller details. Explain to students that they can paint details during the second session once the base colors have dried.

Independent Work:

- Hand out the watercolor paper and ask students to write their name on the back. Remind them to sketch lightly in pencil onto the watercolor paper.
- When students are ready, hand them a watercolor brush so that they can begin. (These paintings may take one or two class sessions to complete.)

Closure:

- Pair students up with a partner from a different table for variety and to ensure that students are responding to a piece of artwork they have not seen before.
- Ask pairs to guess what the most important part of their partner's painting is and see whether they are correct.

Teacher Note: You can also do this activity after the sketching is complete so that students can use their partner's feedback to make modifications to their sketch before they transfer it to their watercolor paper. You can do this activity as a final closure/summative assessment (with a different partner) to see whether a peer can identify their focal point (main idea).

TEACHING THE DETERMINING IMPORTANCE STRATEGY THROUGH READING/LANGUAGE ARTS

Common Core: College and Career Readiness Anchor Standards for Reading

The following reading anchor standards are addressed in the reading lessons in this chapter:

Key ideas and details:
  ° Standard 2: Determine central ideas or themes of a text and analyze their development; summarize the key supporting details and ideas.
Craft and structure:
  ° Standard 5: Analyze the structure of texts, including how specific sentences, paragraphs, and larger portions of the text (e.g., section, chapter, scene, or stanza) relate to each other and the whole.
  ° Standard 6: Assess how point of view or purpose shapes the content and style of a text.
Range of reading and level of text complexity:
  ° Standard 10: Read and comprehend complex literary and informational texts independently and proficiently.

National Reading Standards

The following reading content standards are addressed in the reading lessons in this chapter:

Standard 1: Students read a wide range of print and nonprint texts to build an understanding of texts, of themselves, and of the cultures of the United States and the world; to acquire new information; to respond to the needs and demands of society and the workplace; and for personal fulfillment. Among these texts are fiction and nonfiction, classic and contemporary works.
Standard 3: Students apply a wide range of strategies to comprehend, interpret, evaluate, and appreciate texts. They draw on their prior experience, their interactions

with other readers and writers, their knowledge of word meaning and of other texts, their word identification strategies, and their understanding of textual features (e.g., sound-letter correspondence, sentence structure, context, graphics).

Standard 4: Students adjust their use of spoken, written, and visual language (e.g., conventions, style, vocabulary) to communicate effectively with a variety of audiences and for different purposes.

Standard 11: Students participate as knowledgeable, reflective, creative, and critical members of a variety of literacy communities.

Teacher Note: This reading/language arts lesson uses nonfiction text. Determining importance is a very important skill to develop in order to comprehend nonfiction text.

Mastery Objectives

Students will be able to determine important information in nonfiction text.

Time Frame

Two one-hour sessions

Essential Questions

- How do text features help us to determine what is important in text?
- How does asking questions help us determine what is important in text?
- How does determining important information help us change our thinking?

Materials

- Teacher-made posters or big books, which show examples of text features (e.g., labels, bold-print words, picture captions, fact boxes, headings, pictures, and photographs, table of contents, and index)
- Nonfiction articles from magazines like *Ranger Rick*, *Time for Kids*, and *Scholastic News*
- Nonfiction books on student-generated topics
- Nonfiction big books to show samples of text features
- Digital resources such as www.britannica.com/ or www.timeforkids.com/
- Sticky notes
- 18-inch × 24-inch manila paper
- Pencils and crayons
- Rulers

Session 1: Applying the Strategy to Text

Warm-up/Preassessment: Tell the students that today they will be learning how to determine important information when they are reading nonfiction text. Ask them to think about the art lesson, and have them name ways that artists help their viewers determine what is important in a work of art. Make a connection between what artists and writers do to help viewers/readers focus on the important parts. Explain that just as artists use the elements of art and principles of design (space, color, and emphasis) to help their viewers focus on the important parts of an artwork, authors use text features (bold print, pictures, labels, etc.) in a way to help readers focus on important information. Ask them to tell you what they already know writers do to help their readers decide what the important information is. Chart their responses.

Teacher Modeling:

- Referring to the chart they created during the warm-up, show the students text feature samples from big books or teacher-made posters. Have a sample for each of the following features: table of contents, labels, pictures/photographs, captions, bold-print words, fact boxes, and index. *Teacher Note*: Consider creating separate posters for each text feature, label them, and mount a sample of the text feature on the poster.
- Read an article on a student-generated topic, pointing out the text features the author used.
- Do a think-aloud about what you are learning from the features.
- After reading, tell the students that today they will be reading an article and using the text features to help determine the important information. Then they will use the information to create a teaching poster.
- Model how to create a teaching poster. Consider using the following text features: title, picture with labels, picture with captions, fact box, and bold print.

Session 2: Research and Creating Teaching Posters

Guided Practice/Independent Work:

- Tell students that they will be creating their own teaching posters. Explain that they will first choose an article or section of a book to read on a topic of their choice. Have them use the *text features* to determine the essential information they want to share with readers. During and after reading, they will determine the important information they have learned and what to include in their poster.
- Conference with each student to discuss the student's topic and the important information the student has learned from the text. Ask students how they knew the information was important.

- Have the students create their own posters. Explain that they will need to use text features in their posters to convey the important information they learned about their topic. Provide them with the directions for their posters.
- Ask the students how text features help them determine the essential information in nonfiction text.

Assessment Ideas:

- Note the extent to which students are able to use text features to locate important information.
- When conferencing with the students, ask them to tell you how they knew that the information they learned from the text was important.
- Note whether students are able to use text features in their teaching posters.

RESOURCES

Nonfiction trade books/magazines:

Allaby, M. (2000). *Guide to Weather: A Photographic Journey through the Skies*. New York: Dorling Kindersley.

Pellant, C. (2002). *Smithsonian Handbooks: Rocks & Minerals*. New York: Dorling Kindersley.

Smith, A., and Miles, L. (2010). *The Usborne Book of Astronomy & Space*. Eveleth, MN: Usborne.

Taylor, B. (2002). *Maps and Mapping*. New York: Kingfisher Books.

Nonfiction magazines (e.g., *Ranger Rick, Time for Kids, Scholastic News*)

DK Eyewitness books:

Lambert, D. (2010). *Dinosaur*. New York: Dorling Kindersley.

MacQuitty, M. (2008). *Ocean*. New York: Dorling Kindersley.

Parker, S. (2005). *Fish*. New York: Dorling Kindersley.

English language learner books:

Morgan, A. (2005). *Library*. Easy Stuff Library (ESL) Series. Woodbine, MD: Starting Gate Press.

Morgan, A. (2005). *Trees*. Easy Stuff Library (ESL) Series. Woodbine, MD: Starting Gate Press.

LITERACY BENEFITS

Teaching the strategy of determining importance:

- helps children to navigate nonfiction text by teaching them about the text features authors use to organize information;
- provides children with a format to use to organize their own writing;
- allows children the opportunity to verbalize their thinking; and
- builds on the reader's background knowledge.

Using art to teach how to determine what is important:

- allows children to apply the strategy in a text-free environment;
- creates a culture of learning by allowing all students to share their thinking based on artwork or text;
- provides students with the opportunity to apply and use art vocabulary when discussing works of art; and
- provides students the opportunity to determine what is important in their work, the work of others, and text.

REFLECTION

Using art to teach determining importance can help children understand that artists and writers use techniques to show what is important in their artwork or their text. There are a number of reflections on our experience with the determining importance lesson:

- Students enjoyed viewing artwork and determining what was important in the piece by using the elements of art and principles of design.
- Children demonstrated understanding of how artists stress important features in their work by identifying important parts of the artwork and explaining their thinking.
- Children enjoyed creating their own watercolor pieces and were able to apply the elements of art and principals of design to their own artwork in order to communicate important ideas in their piece.
- In the reading lesson, children were engaged in constructing their teaching posters and were able to use the text features studied in their poster.
- The teaching poster allowed children to apply the important information they learned from reading.

Determining Importance Capture Sheet

Names: _____

Title of Artwork: _____

Artist: _____

Directions: Answer the following questions about your work of art. You can answer using words, pictures, or both.

   1. What is important in this work of art?

   2. How do you know?

Determining Importance Brainstorming Worksheet

Name: _____

Directions: Make a list or draw a quick sketch about four events in your life.

List or draw four events in your life:	
1.	3.
2.	4.
Chose one event above and draw a sketch that emphasizes the most important part of that event.	

SYNTHESIZING

Creating Meaning

Synthesis takes place during and after reading. It is the process of creating a mental plan—a blueprint—for what we're reading, experiencing, or learning—and then continually revising the plan as we recall or encounter new information.

Mosaic of Thought (Keene & Zimmermann, 2007, p. 229)

Synthesis is about organizing the different pieces to create a mosaic, a meaning, a beauty, greater than the sum of each shiny piece.

Mosaic of Thought (Keene & Zimmermann, 2007, p. 229)

Good readers apply the strategy of synthesis throughout the reading process. Synthesizing information helps readers gain the big idea of the piece. Synthesizing involves collecting information during reading and adding it to the schema that is being created in the reader's mind to form a deeper understanding of the text. When children apply this strategy, they collect and organize information over time as the story unfolds and incorporate the information with their own background knowledge to create an understanding of the text. As readers gain new information from the story, a change may occur in their thought processes as they merge the new information with their own current knowledge in order to create a new, greater understanding of the piece. According to Debbie Miller (2002), "Readers monitor overall meaning, important concepts, and themes as they read, understanding that their thinking evolves in the process."

Synthesizing is a necessary strategy for children to develop and apply in their reading in order to be able to identify themes and important messages from the text. It requires children to be active readers and develop an awareness of how their thinking changes and evolves throughout the reading process.

For younger children, synthesizing begins with retelling. According to Debbie Miller, retelling can be a fairly literal recounting of what children have read, learned, and remembered.

Because synthesis is a more complex skill, we recommend these lessons for third through fifth graders or higher.

Why Synthesizing?

Synthesizing is a necessary skill for comprehending text and developing new insights and meaning. Synthesizing:

- requires children to explore their own thinking;
- allows children to change their thinking while reading;
- provides children with the opportunity to reflect on their thinking and share their thoughts with other students;
- deepens comprehension;
- often provides new insights;
- develops active readers;
- requires children to monitor what they are reading;
- enables children to identify the "big ideas" from text; and
- involves applying all the comprehension strategies to gain meaning.

Recommended Texts for Teaching Synthesis

This strategy requires students to be able to collect and organize information while they are reading. Often this requires the reader to adjust his or her thinking throughout the story and may surprise the reader. To teach this strategy, choose texts that slowly unfold the problem and solution of the story. These stories may have a twist or surprise ending.

Abercrombie, B. (1990). *Charlie Anderson*. New York: Aladdin Paperbacks.
Deedy, Carmen Agra. (2009). *14 Cows for America*. Atlanta: Peachtree.
Hazen, B. S. (1983). *Tight Times*. New York: Puffin Books.
Lobel, A. (1990). *Fables*. New York: HarperCollins.
Mortenson, Greg, and Roth, Susan L. (2009). *Listen to the Wind*. New York: Dial Group.
Phillips, J. C. (2009). *Wink: The Ninja Who Wanted to Be Noticed*. New York: Viking.

Why Art and Synthesizing?

The visual arts can be a very powerful tool used to teach the strategy of synthesizing. Using art may help some children to build confidence in using this strategy because most children can say something about a piece of art. Applying the strategy of synthesis to art and reading requires children to look at the various parts of an artwork or text and put them together to make a whole. Using artwork can motivate and engage children because it is visual by nature. Children move from making literal observations of art (What do you notice? What do you see?) to building meaning from a piece of artwork. Synthesizing allows children to move from what they see in the artwork to developing ideas about its meaning.

When students look at a work of art that is abstract, they can begin to interpret it by discussing the elements of art and principles of design (e.g., line, shape, color, balance, rhythm). Students will then examine the parts of the artwork (elements of art) and create meaning using those parts. As they are discussing this work with their peers, they may hear others' observations that might cause them to change their initial idea.

If students are looking at a realistic work of art, they could begin by discussing the characters, setting, and action as well as the elements of art (the parts of the artwork). Then they use their observations of theme, subject matter, mood, and style to create the big ideas of an artwork.

To add even deeper meaning, children can learn about how the artist's background and culture may have influenced the work.

Suggested Pacing for the Synthesis Lessons

This unit of instruction may require additional collaborative planning to determine how each lesson will be taught, and by whom.

Day 1: Introducing the Strategy—Ripple Pond Lesson and Definition of the Strategy
Day 2: Art Lesson—Two Artworks by the Same Artist
Day 3: Reading Lesson—Modeling the Strategy
Day 4: Reading Lesson—Applying the Strategy—Ripple Thinking Sheet
Day 5: Art Lesson—Creating a Synthesis Quilt

TEACHING THE SYNTHESIS STRATEGY THROUGH ART AND READING/LANGUAGE ARTS

Some lessons are adapted from Debbie Miller's *Reading with Meaning*, page 159.

National Visual Arts Standards

The following art content standards are addressed in the art lessons in this chapter:

Content standard 1: Understanding and applying media, techniques, and processes
Content standard 3: Choosing and evaluating a range of subject matter, symbols, and ideas

Content standard 5: Reflecting on and assessing the characteristics and merits of their work and the work of others

Content standard 6: Making connections between visual arts and other disciplines

Common Core: College and Career Readiness Anchor Standards for Reading

The following reading anchor standards are addressed in the reading lessons in this chapter:

Key ideas and details:
- ° Standard 1: Read closely to determine what the text says explicitly and to make logical inferences from it; cite specific textual evidence when writing or speaking to support conclusions drawn from the text.
- ° Standard 2: Determine central ideas or themes of a text and analyze their development; summarize the key supporting details and ideas.
- ° Standard 3: Analyze how and why individuals, events, and ideas develop and interact over the course of a text.

Craft and structure:
- ° Standard 4: Interpret words and phrases as they are used in a text, including determining technical, connotative, and figurative meanings, and analyze how specific word choices shape meaning or tone.
- ° Standard 5: Analyze the structure of texts, including how specific sentences, paragraphs, and larger portions of the text (e.g., section, chapter, scene, or stanza) relate to each other and the whole.

Range of reading and level of text complexity:
- ° Standard 10: Read and comprehend complex literary and informational texts independently and proficiently.

National Reading Standards

The following reading content standards are addressed in the reading lessons in this chapter:

Standard 1: Students read a wide range of print and nonprint texts to build an understanding of texts, of themselves, and of the cultures of the United States and the world; to acquire new information; to respond to the needs and demands of society and the workplace; and for personal fulfillment. Among these texts are fiction and nonfiction, classic and contemporary works.

Standard 3: Students apply a wide range of strategies to comprehend, interpret, evaluate, and appreciate texts. They draw on their prior experience, their interactions with other readers and writers, their knowledge of word meaning and of other texts, their word identification strategies, and their understanding of textual features (e.g., sound-letter correspondence, sentence structure, context, graphics).

Standard 4: Students adjust their use of spoken, written, and visual language (e.g., conventions, style, vocabulary) to communicate effectively with a variety of audiences and for different purposes.

Standard 11: Students participate as knowledgeable, reflective, creative, and critical members of a variety of literacy communities.

Session 1: Ripple Pond Lesson and Definition of the Strategy

Mastery Objective

Students will be able to better understand and define synthesis.

Time Frame

One fifty- to sixty-minute session

Essential Question

How does creating a visual representation help me understand concepts?

Vocabulary

- *Synthesis*: collecting and organizing information over time to develop big ideas
- *Ripple*: waves that expand out, getting larger and larger
- *Change*: to think differently about a topic after gaining more information

Materials

- Pencils
- Pond or large tub of water
- Stones
- Ripple Thinking sheet—create one poster-size sheet (see page 104)

Preassessment: Preassess students' knowledge of the strategy (use pre-/postassessment sheet—see page 105).

Activity—Defining Synthesis:

- Either use a large tub of water or take students to a pond. Present the analogy that synthesis is like the ripples in water.
- Invite students to drop pebbles in the water to observe the ripple.
- Ask the students what they observed. Provide the opportunity for students to discuss their observations with a partner and then share with the whole class.
- Direct students to look at the different rings in the ripple. Point out how the rings get larger and larger as they move outward. Drop the rock in the water multiple times until all students are able to observe the ripples.
- Ask, "How is synthesis like a ripple?" Explain that synthesis in reading is like a ripple.
- Explain that when the rock was dropped in, it started out with one ring. In the beginning, readers have limited information and limited facts/ideas. As the ripple continues moving, it gets bigger and bigger. As readers continue to read, additional facts (information) are gathered and thinking expands.
- Discuss how this ripple analogy might relate to talking about a work of art.
- Ask the students to explain how creating a visual representation of synthesis will help them remember what synthesis means.

Session 2: Art Lesson—Two Works by the Same Artist

Mastery Objectives

- Students will be able to compare the commonalities between two artworks by the same artist.

- Students will be able to synthesize biographical information and visual clues from the artwork to make inferences or predictions about its meaning.

Time Frame

One forty- to fifty-minute class

Essential Question

How does an artist's background (life) influence his or her work?

Vocabulary

Quick sketch: a drawing that is created quickly using no details

Materials

- Two reproductions of artwork by the same artist. Some suggestions for artists are below:
  - ° Jacob Lawrence
  - ° Pablo Picasso
  - ° Vincent Van Gogh
  - ° Georgia O'Keeffe
  - ° Horace Pippin
  - ° Faith Ringgold
- Chart paper
- Art Ripple Thinking Sheet (see page 106)
- Biography or background information about the artist you choose—the "Getting to Know the World's Greatest Artists" series is extremely kid friendly. For a list of all the artists in the "Getting to Know" series please visit www.gettingtoknow.com/artists.htm.
- Background information about the artist's time period

Guided Discussion:

- Display a work of art. While students look at the work, ask them to describe what they see. (List responses on chart paper.)
- Guide students into using the elements of art and principles of design to discuss what they see (e.g., color, line, texture, space, form).

- Ask students to talk about subject matter, mood, and setting of the artwork.
- Display another artwork created by the same artist, and post it next to the first piece. Ask students to describe again what they see. This time, circle anything that is similar about both artworks.
- Model how to draw a quick sketch of their thinking. A quick sketch is rapidly drawing out ideas and observations without great detail. (See chapter 3 for a quick sketch template.)
- Ask students to fill out the top of the Art Ripple Thinking Sheet.
- Share some biographical information about the artist (e.g., book, article).
- Ask students to use that information to fill in the bottom of the worksheet. Provide time for students to synthesize (develop new thinking) the new information. Encourage them to discuss their new thinking about the artist now that they have learned more about him or her.
- Facilitate a group discussion that allows students the opportunity to share their thoughts and discoveries about the artist/artwork with the class.

Session 3: Applying the Strategy—Ripple Thinking Sheet

Mastery Objectives

- Students will better understand and define synthesis.
- Students will be able to retell or synthesize what they have read.
- Students will respond to texts in a variety of ways (oral, visual, written).
- Students will share, discuss, and interpret what they have read.
- Students will use knowledge of the story elements to make decisions about the meaning of the passage, chapter, or book.
- Students will use a preassessment graphic organizer (on page 105) to record their thinking and process the big ideas in a text.

Time Frame

One to two fifty-minute sessions

Essential Question

What do good readers do to deepen their understanding of what they have read?

Vocabulary

Quick sketch: a drawing that is created quickly using no details

Materials

- Book: *Charlie Anderson* by Barbara Abercrombie (or see alternative text ideas in the resources on page 92)
- Poster-size Ripple Thinking Sheet
- Teacher model of quick sketch from previous lesson
- Pencils
- Paper
- Ripple Thinking Sheet (see page 104)
- Books that slowly unfold a problem and a solution (e.g., *Tight Times* by Barbara Shook Hazen)

Model (Think-Aloud): Discuss with the students that they will be using the synthesis reading strategy by drawing quick sketches to help organize their thinking, retell the part that was read, and create meaning from the text.

- Explain that synthesis involves retelling what you have read, understanding story elements, making connections, making inferences, drawing conclusions, and making new meaning.
- Discuss how the Ripple Thinking Sheet allows students to create quick sketches during specific parts of a story. Remind students that synthesis is like a ripple; thinking starts small and gets bigger and bigger.
- Read the story *Charlie Anderson* by Barbara Abercrombie. Stop at predetermined spots throughout the book to model how a reader collects information throughout the reading process. For example, stop on page 4 (after the cat is introduced) and model what is known about the cat so far.
- Model how sketching what you were thinking about the facts helps you retell, infer, synthesize, and organize your thinking. (*Note*: The teacher may model this strategy alone or with another teacher/partner. If done with a partner, share out loud how your thinking has changed over time.)
- Modeling includes constant thinking out loud. Tell students what you were thinking and how you got to that point. Talk about how the Ripple Thinking Sheet is a good way to record your ideas. It may be used to retell the story, to remember facts, and to show how thinking changes over time. Pose questions that ask the students to discuss how looking at the parts helped them to discover the big picture of the story.

Guided Practice:

- Read the story *Tight Times* by Barbara Shook Hazen. Stop after page 2 and have the students fill in the first two rows of their Ripple Thinking Sheet.

- Break the students into groups of three or four and have them share and discuss their responses. Stop on page 8 and then again at the end of the book until the second and third rows have been filled in. Make sure the students understand that these are supposed to be quick sketches, not a finished product. The Ripple Thinking Sheet will help students visually organize the facts they read and record what they were thinking as they read.
- As a group, have students reflect on their new thinking. Ask them questions like:
  a. What do you think the author wanted you to learn?
  b. In what ways has this story made you think about something new?
  c. How have you broadened your understanding of yourself or others?

Sharing: Have each group share its thinking with the class.

Closure:

- Remind students about seeing the ripple in the pond or tub of water. Ask students to describe how a ripple is like synthesis.
- Review the essential question and the definition of synthesis.
  ° Essential Question: What do good readers do to deepen their understanding of what they have read?
  ° Synthesis Definition: collecting and organizing information over time to develop big ideas.

Assessment Idea:

- Ask students to take out their pre-/postassessment sheet and answer the question at the bottom.
- Draw or write what synthesis means to you. (See the web worksheet on page 105.)

Session 4: Art—Creating a Synthesis Quilt

Mastery Objectives

- Students will use their Ripple Thinking Sheet to recall/retell the story.
- Students will create a final drawing of the author's big picture or central message for the story.

Time Frame

One fifty-minute session

Essential Question

How does thinking about the different parts of the story help to create the "big picture?"

Art Vocabulary

- *Elements of art*: line, color, shape, texture, form, space, and value
- *Principles of design*: pattern, repetition, contrast, balance, rhythm, movement, unity, and emphasis
- *Mood*: a particular state of mind or feeling

Materials

- Drawing paper (cut square paper for quilt pieces 9-inch × 9-inch, 10-inch × 10-inch, 11-inch × 11-inch, or 12-inch × 12-inch—depending on how big you want the quilt to be)
- Pencils and erasers
- Drawing materials (colored pencils, oil pastels, crayons, markers)
- Watercolor
- Brushes
- Water containers

Preassessment:

- Review the meaning of synthesis.
- Using the Ripple Thinking Sheet, ask students to retell the story with a partner and discuss their new thinking.

Model (Think-Aloud):

- Tell students they will be making a "synthesis quilt," and explain how all their pictures will be put together to create a paper quilt. Explain to students the concept of a patchwork quilt. (Each block of fabric is different, and you attach the pieces together to create a blanket or quilt.)
- Show examples of quilts.
- Demonstrate how to draw a mental picture of the story. Refer to your Ripple Thinking Sheet.
- Model how to turn a quick sketch into a finished work of art.
- Model how to use watercolor to add color, contrast, and emphasis to show mood.

Independent Practice (Drawing): Pass out materials. Remind students that this time they need to draw, not sketch, their ideas. Have them use the synthesis strategy to draw their new understanding of the story.

Creating the Quilt: Put the artwork on banner paper to create a story synthesis quilt.

Lesson Extensions:

- Students can help put the artwork on banner paper to create a story synthesis quilt.
- Students can create a shared writing about the quilt that is displayed next to the quilt.

RESOURCES

Books

Edwards, B. (2012). *Drawing on the Right Side of the Brain*. New York: Tarcher.

Venezia, M. (1988). *Getting to Know the Artist: Pablo Picasso*. Danbury, CT: Children's Press.

Venezia, M. (1989). *Getting to Know the Artist: Vincent Van Gogh*. Danbury, CT: Children's Press.

Venezia, M. (1994). *Getting to Know the Artist: Georgia O'Keeffe*. Danbury, CT: Children's Press.

Venezia, M. (2000). *Getting to Know the Artist: Jacob Lawrence*. Danbury, CT: Children's Press.

Venezia, M. (2008a). *Getting to Know the Artist: Faith Ringgold*. Danbury, CT: Children's Press.

Venezia, M. (2008b). *Getting to Know the Artist: Horace Pippin*. Danbury, CT: Children's Press.

Artists

- Jacob Lawrence
- Pablo Picasso
- Vincent Van Gogh
- Georgia O'Keeffe
- Horace Pippin
- Faith Ringgold

LITERACY BENEFITS

The synthesizing lessons provide children the opportunity to:

- create a deeper understanding of what is being read;
- verbalize their thinking;
- create a culture of learning by allowing them to share their thinking based on the artwork or text;
- develop listening comprehension skills;
- hear book language through the read-alouds;
- use art and reading vocabulary.

REFLECTION

There are a number of reflections on our experience with this synthesis unit.

- Students were introduced to the strategy through multiple modalities to accommodate various learners.
- Students were engaged in the lessons.
- Students enjoyed going outside and observing a real ripple. This opportunity allowed students to attach meaning to the synthesis strategy by seeing a concrete example in nature. The movement and the flow of this lesson provided opportunities for movement and real-life experiences for the kinesthetic and visual learners.
- Quick sketching allowed students the freedom to capture their thinking without having to complete a finished product and record their thinking through pictures versus writing.
- Stopping students at predetermined parts of the story allowed students to process their thinking and document how it changed over time.
- The Ripple Thinking Sheet allowed students the opportunity to break down their thinking into smaller steps that they used to develop the big picture.
- Breaking down the steps was key in teaching children the strategy of synthesis.
- The Ripple Thinking Sheet acted as a tool to develop metacognition.
- Children enjoyed creating art by using the big ideas in the story to create their quilt square, which reinforced the synthesis strategy visually.
- Children deepened their understanding that art and reading offer multiple levels of comprehension.

Synthesis Ripple Thinking

Name: _____ Date: _____

Story Title: _____

Facts ⃝	Thinking ⃝
Facts ◎	Thinking ◎
Facts ◉	Thinking ◉
Facts ◉	Thinking ◉

Day 1: Synthesis Lesson

Name: _____ Date: _____

Preassessment for Synthesis Strategy
What do you already know about the strategy of synthesis? You may use words and/or pictures in your answer.
Postassessment for Synthesis Strategy
What have you learned about synthesis? You may use words and/or pictures in your answer.

🎨 🎨 🎨 🎨 🎨 🎨 🎨 🎨 🎨 🎨 🎨 🎨 🎨

CHAPTER 6

Art Ripple Thinking Sheet

Name: _____ Date: _____

Directions: Use the elements of art and principles of design to discuss what you see and what it might mean about the artwork. Write or sketch your answers.

◎ What do you see?	◎ What does it mean?

Read background information about the artist and/or time period.

◎ What is your new thinking?

🎨 🎨 🎨 🎨 🎨 🎨 🎨 🎨 🎨 🎨 🎨 🎨

BIBLIOGRAPHY

Abercrombie, B. (1990). *Charlie Anderson*. New York: Aladdin Paperbacks.

Allaby, M. (2000). *Guide to Weather: A Photographic Journey through the Skies*. New York: Dorling Kindersley.

Anno, M. (1978). *Anno's Journey*. Cleveland, OH: William Collins & World.

Baker, J. (2004). *Home*. New York: Greenwillow Books.

Bang, M. (1980). *The Grey Lady and the Strawberry Snatcher*. Cincinnati, OH: Four Winds Press.

Baylor, B., and Parnall, P. (1998). *The Table Where the Rich People Sit*. New York: Aladdin.

Bryant, J. (2005). *Georgia's Bones*. Grand Rapids, MI: Eerdmans Books for Young Readers.

Condra, E. (1994). *See the Ocean*. Nashville, TN: Ideals.

Deedy, Carmen Agra. (2009). *14 Cows for America*. Atlanta: Peachtree.

DePaola, T. (1978). *Pancakes for Breakfast*. Troy, MO: Harcourt Brace Jovanovich.

Dickins, R. (2005). *Usborne: The Children's Book of Art*. London: Usborne.

Dole, J. A., Duffy, G. G., Roehler, L. R., and Pearson, P. D. (1991). Moving from the old to the new: Research on reading comprehension instruction. *Review of Education Research, 61*(2), 239–64.

Duffy, G. G., Roehler, L. R., and Herrmann, B. A. (1988). Modeling mental processes helps poor readers become strategic readers. *Reading Teacher, 41*(8), 762–67.

Duffy, G. G., Roehler, R. R., Sivan, E., Rackliffe, G., Book, C., Meloth, M. S., . . . Bassiri, D. (1987). Effects of explaining the reasoning associated with using strategies. *Reading Research Quarterly, 22*(3), 347–68.

Edwards, B. (2012). *Drawing on the Right Side of the Brain*. New York: Tarcher.

Fielding, L., and Pearson, D. (1994). Reading comprehension: What works. *Educational Leadership, 45*(3), 7–13.

Fiske, E. B. (1999). *Champions of Change: The Impact of the Arts on Learning*. President's Committee on the Arts and the Humanities; Arts Education Partnership, Washington, DC.

Foa, M., and Philip, N. (Eds.). (1995). *Songs Are Thoughts: Poems of the Inuit*. New York: Orchard Books.

Gallager, M., and Pearson, D. (1983). The instruction of reading comprehension. *Contemporary Education Psychology, 8*, 317–44.

Hall, D. (Ed). (1999). *The Oxford Illustrated Book of American Children's Poems*. New York: Oxford University Press.

Harvey, S., and Goudvis, A. (2007). *Strategies That Work*. Portland, ME: Stenhouse.

Harvey, S., McAuliffe, S., Benson, L., Cameron, W., Kempton, S., Lusche, P., . . . Weaver, J. (1996, December). Teacher-researchers study the process of synthesizing in six primary classrooms. *Language Arts, 73*, 564–74.

Hazen, B. S. (1983). *Tight Times*. New York: Puffin Books.

Hoyt, L. (2008). *Revisit/Reflect/Retell*. Portsmouth, NH: Heinemann.

Huang, T. (1992). *In the Eyes of Cats*. New York: Henry Holt.

Keene, E. O., and Zimmermann, S. (2007). *Mosaic of Thought*. Portsmouth, NH: Heinemann.

Lambert, D. (2010). *Dinosaur*. New York: Dorling Kindersley.

Lobel, A. (1990). *Fables*. New York: HarperCollins.

MacLachlan, P., and Charest, E. (2010). *I Didn't Do It*. New York: Katherine Tegen.

MacQuitty, M. (2008). *Ocean*. New York: Dorling Kindersley.

Mantione, R. D., and Smead, S. (2003). *Weaving through Words: Using the Arts to Teach Reading Comprehension Strategies*. Newark, DE: International Reading Association.

McCully, E. A. (2001). *Four Hungry Kittens*. New York: Penguin Putnam.

Miller, D. (2002). *Reading with Meaning: Teaching Comprehension in the Primary Grades*. Portland, ME: Stenhouse.

Morgan, A. (2005). *Library*. Easy Stuff Library (ESL) Series. Woodbine, MD: Starting Gate Press.

Morgan, A. (2005). *Trees*. Easy Stuff Library (ESL) Series. Woodbine, MD: Starting Gate Press.

Mortenson, Greg, and Roth, Susan L. (2009). *Listen to the Wind*. New York: Dial Group.

Olaleye, I. (2001). *The Distant Talking Drum*. Honesdale, PA: Wordsong.

Parker, S. (2005). *Fish*. New York: Dorling Kindersley.

Pellant, C. (2002). *Smithsonian Handbooks: Rocks & Minerals*. New York: Dorling Kindersley.

Phillips, J. C. (2009). *Wink: The Ninja Who Wanted to Be Noticed*. New York: Viking.

Pink, D. (2006). *A Whole New Mind*. New York: Riverhead Books.

Pinkney, J. (2006). *The Little Red Hen*. New York: Penguin Group.

Raczka, B. (2002). *No One Saw—Ordinary Things through the Eyes of an Artist*. Minneapolis, MN: Millbrook Press.

Rampersaud, L. B. (2006). *Bubble and Squeak*. Tarrytown, NY: Marshall Cavendish.

Roessel, D., and Rampersad, A. (2006). *Poetry for Young People: Langston Hughes*. New York: Sterling.

Rylant, C. (1988). *All I See*. New York: Orchard Books.

Sabol, R. (2010). *No Child Left Behind: A Study of Its Impact on Art Education*. Reston, VA: National Art Education Association.

Sage, A. (1998). *The Treasury of Children's Poetry*. London: Hutchinson Children's Books.

Shannon, G. (1996). *Spring, A Haiku Story*. New York: Greenwillow Books.

Smith, A., and Miles, L. (2010). *The Usborne Book of Astronomy & Space*. Eveleth, MN: Usborne.

Tafuri, N. (1987). *Do Not Disturb*. New York: Greenwillow Books.

Taylor, B. (2002). *Maps and Mapping*. New York: Kingfisher Books.

Thomas, J. C. (1993). *Brown Honey in Broomwheat Tea*. New York: HarperCollins.

Venezia, M. (1988). *Getting to Know the Artist: Pablo Picasso*. Danbury, CT: Children's Press.

——. (1989). *Getting to Know the Artist: Vincent Van Gogh*. Danbury, CT: Children's Press.

——. (1994). *Getting to Know the Artist: Georgia O'Keeffe*. Danbury, CT: Children's Press.

——. (2000). *Getting to Know the Artist: Jacob Lawrence*. Danbury, CT: Children's Press.

——. (2004). *Getting to Know the Artist: Winslow Homer*. Danbury, CT: Children's Press.

——. (2008a). *Getting to Know the Artist: Faith Ringgold*. Danbury, CT: Children's Press.

——. (2008b). *Getting to Know the Artist: Horace Pippin*. Danbury, CT: Children's Press.

Worth, V. (1996). *All the Small Poems and Fourteen More*. New York: Farrar, Straus and Giroux.

Yolen, J. (2000). *Color Me a Rhyme*. Honesdale, PA: Wordsong.

Zimmermann, S., and Hutchins, C. (2003). *7 Keys to Comprehension*. New York: Three Rivers Press.

ABOUT THE AUTHORS

Jennifer Klein has worked as an elementary classroom teacher, gifted and talented teacher, staff development teacher, and teacher trainer for Montgomery County Public Schools in Rockville, Maryland. She is currently working as a reading specialist for MCPS. She holds a master of education degree and a bachelor of science degree from the University of Maryland, College Park. In 2003, Jennifer received the Jr. Great Books Great Teacher Award, for her work with integrating Jr. Great Books with the social studies curriculum.

Jennifer is interested in literacy and the arts, and teaching writing to children. Over the past several years, she has brought her love of literacy and art together to create after-school and summer workshops for children, including the Artist/Readers' Workshop and the Artist/Writers' Workshop, and has taught at the Rehoboth Art League in Rehoboth, Delaware. She is a member of the National Art Education Association (NAEA), and has presented at county, state, and national conferences. She lives in Bethesda, Maryland.

Elizabeth (Lisa) Stuart taught elementary art for nine years and has been the content specialist for art, theatre, and dance for Montgomery County Public Schools in Rockville, Maryland, for the past five years. She received her bachelor of science in art education degree from the University of Maryland, College Park; her master of arts in education degree from the Maryland Institute College of Art (MICA) in Baltimore, Maryland; and her certificate in supervision and administration from the University of Maryland, College Park. Lisa has traveled extensively throughout the world and in 2006 was awarded a Japan Fulbright scholarship.

In 2009, Lisa received the Eastern Region Elementary Art Teacher of the Year award, and in 2012, Lisa received the Maryland Art Educator of the Year award from the National Art Education Association (NAEA). She has presented at numerous state and national conventions on various topics concerning curriculum, assessment, and instruction. She loves to find ways for children to use art to deepen their understanding of other subjects and believes that all children can access the same level of understanding in different ways. Using art is one such way. Lisa lives in Silver Spring, Maryland, with her husband, Dan, a metal sculptor, and her two children, Caitlin and Colin.

The authors can be reached at www.teachreadingusingart.com.